The
Girl
Guide

The Girl Guide

Finding Your Place in a Mixed-Up World

Christine Fonseca

PRUFROCK PRESS INC.
WACO, TEXAS

Dedication

Dedicated to my girls, Fabiana and Erika, for reminding me that there are no limits to what we can dream or become.

Prufrock Press Inc.
P.O. Box 8813
Waco, TX 76714-8813
Phone: (800) 998-2208
Fax: (800) 240-0333
http://www.prufrock.com

Table of Contents

Acknowledgements

Being a parent of two girls, I am always looking for ways to help them become strong, independent women. This book afforded me an opportunity to not only write something specifically for them, but connect with other amazing and dynamic young women and bring their stories forward as continued sources of inspiration. That said, this book was not created without the help of an entire team of amazing people.

First, this book would never have been written without the daily support and inspiration from my husband, Dirck, and my girls, Fabiana and Erika. Not only did they keep the household running every time I went away to my writing cave, but they also supplied a constant source of courage and inspiration to bring this book to life.

Next, I couldn't have shaped the ideas and the book without the encouragement and guidance of my editor, Lacy Compton. She has been a never-ending sea of support, and I am so blessed to have her in my life. The team at Prufrock Press gave substance to my ideas and helped me create something amazing.

My writing partner, Michelle McLean, an inspirational woman in her own right, helped point out the flaws and push me to dig deeper and go bigger.

There were so many amazing girls and women who shared a piece of themselves to make this book more than a few words on a page. Thanks to all of you, the pages of this book have come to life in a way that inspires. In particular, thank you to Jessi Kirby, Melodye Shore, Elle Horne, Heather McCorkle, Abby Mohaupt, Mona Chicks, Rebekah Graham, S. R. Johannes, Stasia Ward Kehoe, Paula Earl, Erin Hastedt, B. E. Sanderson, Lisa Rivero, Gretchen McNeil, and Jen Merrill—your Note to Self contributions are so very special.

So many parents and kids contributed to this book through letters, interviews, Skype sessions, focus groups, and conversations. More than 300 people from 30 states and five countries participated in some way. I am so humbled by your willingness to share your stories and thoughts. You are all amazing tributes to what it means to be resilient and strong.

My writing wouldn't be anything without the readers, bloggers, and online community that has welcomed me into the fold and shared themselves with me. Thank you for allowing me to continue to bring you the kinds of stories, books, and articles I want to write.

Finally, a special thank you to the two most inspirational women in my life—my grandmother, Maria Tumilty, and my mom, Judi Warren. Although you are both no longer present in my world, you are part of my daily thoughts and prayers. I see you in the faces of my children and the strength in their eyes. From you both, I learned what it means to be a strong, powerful woman. I learned never to buy into the stigma and stereotypes of women in our culture. And I learned that my only limits come from me. I owe you more than you will ever know.

—Christine Fonseca

Introduction

Gabby Douglas, Kyla Ross, Adzo Kpossi, Missy Franklin—what do these amazing athletes of the 2012 Olympics have in common? They are all girls 17 and under. Together with lesser known teens, they have redefined the image of young, strong, and accomplished girls for generations to come. Each one of them has learned to set goals, overcome adversity, and focus on their dreams.

Which is where this book comes in.

More than a book about growing up strong, *The Girl Guide: Finding Your Place in a Mixed-Up World* is all about finding your own unique place in the world, your authentic voice.

Now, I know that life can be hard. There are expectations from everyone to act a certain way, fill a certain role. There are even expectations about *not* listening to those who tell you how to act. Sometimes there are things that happen that send your life spiraling out of control, things you can't foresee. Sometimes you make bad choices that lead to horrible consequences, throwing you completely out of balance. And sometimes it feels like all of the dreams you had when you were a young child move out of reach as you get older.

Maybe you feel like you have to fit in with a certain group and act a certain way just to secure your future. And maybe you think you have to "buck the system" because that's what it means to be strong.

Guess what? Strength and resiliency are actually something different. They're about making your own definition of your life. They're about exploring your options, developing your talents, and not allowing the various barriers life may throw your way stop you from achieving your dreams.

And they're also about allowing those dreams to morph and change just as you grow and develop.

My hope for you as you read this book is that you begin to hear and listen to the voice deep inside—the one that holds your authentic self. The one that is already confident and secure.

In the following pages you'll read stories and strategies for cultivating your own unique self. You'll read about girls who have overcome the odds and achieved more than was expected. You'll get strategies and projects that will help you discover your own unique voice in this crazy, noisy world!

Starting On Your Personal Journey

This book was designed to be used as a guide, a workbook, and a source of inspiration. Each part starts with an introduction and short quiz. Take the quizzes often, as your answers will change over time. Each chapter contains a What Would You Do? scenario that brings the concepts into the real world, and a Note to Self section that shares some advice from other strong young women and successful adults who have found their unique voices.

Additionally, the chapters include quotes from other teens, tools (not rules) to help guide you on your quest, and activities to help you redefine normal for yourself.

My hope is that you will use this book as you need it—and use it often.

Things You May Need

The activities, quizzes, and worksheets throughout the book can be completed in many ways. They can be done in the book if you'd like. One particularly helpful tool is a journal. These can be the little journals you use for school or something bigger. You can do the activities and worksheets in the journal so you can create your own personal memoir of this journey toward your authentic self.

Other useful items include index cards, glue sticks, pictures, colored pencils or pens, and anything else you can use with the various activities to make them your own. You can even take the activities into the digital age, using Photoshop, Pinterest, Glogster, video software, and more. Remember, this journey is all about you—so be as creative as you want to be.

Adding Your Voice

If you find this book helpful to you and want to offer up your own story or tools for other young women, please do! I'm always looking to bring more advice, tools, and inspiration to girls just like you. Just e-mail me at christine@christinefonseca.com, and share your stories. It's one of the best ways to give back to others.

A Word to Parents

Growing up is a challenging job—and growing up strong and resilient in today's fast-paced and turbulent world can be even more challenging. That's where this book comes in. Packed with quotes, stories, and life tools, *The Girl Guide: Finding Your Place in a Mixed-Up World* is designed to help girls find their own unique voice in our chaotic and often noisy world.

The Girl Guide focuses on the principles of resiliency, including social acceptance, self-efficacy, and emotional balance. Additionally, it provides specific strategies and tools for some of the more common issues facing girls today, including relational aggression, staying safe online, school performance, social adjustment, and the mother-daughter connection.

Use this book to address various concerns as they come up. Or read it first and then share it with your girls. Either way, be sure to talk about the information and advice with your teens. Use the ideas as a springboard to open the lines of communication. And if you find something particularly helpful, shoot me a note and let me know.

I wish you much success in being the coach your girls need as they progress through their years and embrace everything it means to be strong young women.

Part 1

The Journey Begins

Understanding how to develop your authentic self begins with understanding who you are in the first place. The upcoming chapters discuss how to discover what it means to be "you," including your strengths and difficulties. The worksheets and quizzes give you the tools to discover your strengths and opportunities for growth, establish goals, and develop healthy lifestyle choices that can put you on a path toward your dreams.

The chapters also begin to delve into the concept of resiliency. Defined by Merriam-Webster as "the ability to recover or adjust to change," the attributes of resiliency can make the difference between falling short of your goals and learning to pick yourself up and push through the hard times.

Before we begin the journey toward your authentic selves, I've got a little quiz to get you thinking about your own authenticity. Answer the five true/false questions before reading through this section.

The Girl Guide

Quiz #1

My Journey Begins

1. I know how to set goals that are responsible and measurable.

   ☐ True   ☐ False

2. I think it is more important to be myself than to have a lot of friends.

   ☐ True   ☐ False

3. I practice healthy habits like getting enough sleep and eating properly most days.

   ☐ True   ☐ False

4. I understand the importance of exercising and being relaxed.

   ☐ True   ☐ False

5. I have a good sense of my strengths, as well as the areas I need to improve.

   ☐ True   ☐ False

Come back and retake the quiz anytime you feel a little disconnected from yourself. Then revisit the activities and tools presented in the chapters, just to refine your skills.

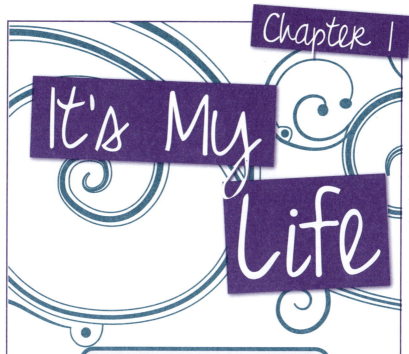

Chapter 1

It's My Life

> The best advice I've ever received? Be yourself.
> If someone else doesn't like it, that's on them.
> You just worry about being true to who you
> are. —Maya, age 16

Every journey begins with a map and supplies, including an inner journey. And you can't create a map until you know where you are right now and where you would like to go. Over the next several pages, you are going to learn how to determine where you are and begin to make your supply list of what you may need on the journey toward your authentic self. But first, let's start with a little scenario.

What Would You Do?

You have a lot on your plate—school, sports and other extracurricular activities, taking care of your little sisters while your parents work. It's a lot of responsibility. You're tired, stressed, and always feel like you are fighting off a cold.

After several months of this grueling schedule, you really want to talk with your parents about lightening your load a little bit. But you don't want to disappoint anyone. Nor do you want to sound like a burden to them.

What do you do? Tell your parents how you feel? Suck it up and just deal with your schedule, regardless of how you feel? Let yourself get sick and have your physical health communicate your needs? Just drop out of things without telling anyone?

Take a moment and write down what you would do to navigate through this challenging situation.

Who Am I?

As I mentioned at the beginning of this chapter, starting on a new journey begins with a map. And the only way to create a map is to know both where you are and where you want to go. Easier said than done at times.

It's hard to really understand who you are at your core. Sure, you can look into a mirror and make judgments about your looks. You can use words like tall or short, blond or brunette, lean or heavy, as ways to describe what you look like. But these descriptions only involve your physical attributes, not the essence of "you" inside.

Now, I'm not saying that physical form isn't important. I would be lying if I told you that human beings don't make judgments about you based on physical attributes. And there are a lot of books and magazines that address the latest fashion and beauty trends. But not this book.

This book is about going deeper, beyond the physical descriptions we may use for ourselves and into the inner attributes that shape how we act and the decisions we make.

It has to do with the you on the inside.

How do you get to know her? How do you discover that authentic self and make a place for her in the world? Those are the questions we will explore in this book.

It starts with taking stock of some of the personality attributes you may have. Things like whether or not you enjoy school, the types of friends you enjoy, and your hobbies. Take a look at the Who Am I? worksheet and work through the various attributes listed, indicating which ones describe you and which ones do not.

The Girl Guide

Worksheet #1 — Who Am I?

Directions: Take a moment and read each statement, indicating if you agree or disagree.

Skill	I agree	I disagree
I'm a good listener.		
People say I am fun to be with.		
I have a lot of friends.		
I like to be active.		
I prefer reading to most sports.		
I would rather draw than read.		
Math is my favorite subject.		
I am a strong student.		
I enjoy spending time with my family.		
When my friends and I argue, I am usually the one to make things better.		
When I am mad, I stay mad for a long time.		
I do my homework on time most nights.		
I like to be involved in a lot of activities.		

Now, take a moment and write a few words or sentences to describe yourself based on those attributes.

This list is by no means exhaustive. It is merely a starting point. After you've worked through the list, take a few minutes to write a description of yourself in your journal or at the end of the worksheet. Try to stay away from any physical descriptions of yourself and focus on the core attributes of the inner you. Think, too, about your quirks, habits, and things that make you unique. For example, one girl I spoke with said she loves to analyze everything, making literal analyses about nonliteral statements—all as a way to drive her friends a little crazy. It is her own unique quirk and something her friends identify as completely her.

Once you have a good, working description for who you are right now, begin the next section and start to plot out where you want to go.

Dream Big

Although you certainly don't need to have a destination in mind when setting off on an exciting journey, it is helpful if you have some idea as to the direction you'd like to go in. With inner journeys, that means having some idea as to your future dreams.

When developing your dreams, there are no limitations. Don't let an inner voice of doubt get in the way of your fantasies. Don't think about the barriers that could prevent you from the dreams. Don't limit yourself in any way. There will be time to manage the dreams and deal with making them realistic, but not here. Not now.

This is the opportunity to explore all of the possibilities of your life. Eleanor Roosevelt and Anaïs Nin are both known for their ability to inspire. They spoke of living a courageous life, of dreaming and achieving.

Dreaming unabashed takes courage. But so does living an authentic life.

To help you get in touch with your deepest dreams, I've included a little activity designed to release your inner dreamer. Remember, the best way to approach this is without your inner editor—the voice that tells you all of the reasons why you can't achieve something. There is a place for that voice of reason, but not yet. Not here.

> *I really want to open a cupcakery one day. I've got a menu all picked out, an idea of my logo, and even some idea of how I'd want my store to look. Next, I'm going to research how to get started. Why not, right? What have I got to lose?* —Erika, age 12

Take some time and really explore all of the crazy, wild things you would one day like to do and then do the Dream Poster activity. Repeat this activity often, as you will find that your dreams will expand as you begin to fully embrace the inner you. You might even set up a bulletin board for your dreams in your room—something you can change easily and often as your goals and dreams change.

One more important note—sometimes it is really hard to hear your inner voice and get in touch with your dreams. Maybe your life is filled with hardship. Maybe you have to deal with situations that make dreaming of a happy life really difficult. Maybe you are too bound by expectations and other things to even know what you want for yourself.

In these cases, I still want you to try to make a dream poster. Make your first poster about the expectations, if that is what quiets that inner voice. Or pretend you are someone else, and make a poster about that person's dreams. Just try the activity.

Dream Poster

1. Using your journal or something similar, list some of the things you like to do.

2. Find or draw pictures that reflect your list. For example, if you like to paint and draw, maybe find a picture of an artist's easel.

3. Make a collage of the pictures.

4. Under the collage, write a goal for your self-something you would like to achieve.

5. Date the collage.

6. Every few months, reflect back on the collage. Do you need to add to it? Or make a new collage?

7. Try to keep a current collage of your dreams and goals to serve as a reminder of where you want to go!

8. For even more fun, use PowerPoint, Photoshop, Glogster, or similar technology to "create" a collage of you living your dream. Import this collage to your phone, tablet, or any place you can see it daily.

9. DREAM BIG!

Learn to listen for that inner voice. Sometimes it will come while you sleep. Sometimes it will be nothing more than a random thought or whisper. And sometimes it's merely you noticing a color or song that you like. Pay attention to these hints of the you that lives within. Eventually she will make herself known to you. As you begin to pay attention to her, she will guide you to parts of yourself that have been silent.

The Journey

Now that you have the beginnings of a definition of where you are and where you would eventually like to go, it's time to map out a path to get there. What's one way to do this? Goals.

When setting goals, it is important to both set the overall goal and determine how you might achieve the goal—the baby steps needed to go in the right direction.

Now, this may seem a little daunting, especially if your dreams are big and fabulous. Never fear, this is still just an exercise in working toward your dreams. You don't need to edit your aspirations or curtail the goals. This is just about learning how to walk in the direction of your dreams.

In the next worksheet, I want you to practice setting a few goals. For this exercise, I want you to set little goals that you can achieve over the next several weeks. The best goals are the ones that are clear; ones that you can measure in some way. The example I use in the chart is a small goal of "pass my math final." It is a goal that can be achieved in a semester. It is measurable and clear.

In order to achieve my goal, there are a few steps I will need to do to get me to travel in the right direction. One is studying math nightly. Another could be reworking any errors I make on tests or

Worksheet #2: Setting Goals

Directions: Think about the goals for each area, then create a plan and time frame for accomplishing each goal.

Area	Plan	Time Frame
School Goal #1 Pass my math final	– Study for 15 minutes a night – Redo any problems on the quiz I got wrong – Ask my teacher for help if I get confused	3 months
School Goal #1		
School Goal #2		
Personal Goal #1		
Personal Goal #2		
Long-Term Goal #1		
Long-Term Goal #2		

asking my teacher for help. Any of these ideas will help me move toward my goal of passing my math final.

In addition to determining activities needed in order to achieve the goal, it is helpful to establish a timeline. This is a way to hold ourselves accountable and not allow the day-in/day-out routines of life derail us on our journey.

Take some time and create some goals for school and home, using the goal-setting worksheet. Be sure to think about a few activities for each goal that can help you move toward achieving it. Revisit your goals regularly and adjust things as you and your dreams change.

Goal setting is something that takes a little practice, but can help frame and focus your life and help you achieve things you may not have ever thought possible. And goals can help give you a framework for your courage—they can help turn the big ideas you may have for your life into something manageable.

So practice writing small goals and develop this into a habit you can use when approaching some of the bigger goals you may have for your life.

Becoming a goal-writing/goal-following expert is a great way to help you continue on the journey toward your dreams. It enables you to experience small victories along the way. It's important to celebrate these small victories. Life can be hard at times. There are more reasons to give up on your dreams than there are reasons to pursue them. But goals can help you stay focused and remember what it is you want to achieve.

And both goals and dreams can help you stay in touch with the inner you.

Note to Self: Work Hard

Success at anything takes hard work. Just because you're good at something, or it's your dream, doesn't make you an automatic success at it. To truly succeed you have to push harder than is comfortable. Work longer than you want to. Experience setbacks and decide to keep going. It's not something that's easily won. It's something you work at, again and again, because it matters to you. —Jessi Kirby

This chapter was just the beginning, a chance to experience some of your inner dreams and practice a particular strategy designed to help you as you begin to carve your own unique niche in the world.

As the opening scenario illustrated, sometimes we just take on too many things at once. Our dreams are big, the expectations we have for ourselves combine with the expectations others have, and we become overwhelmed by it all. In the next chapters, we will deal with managing expectations, setting boundaries, and developing resiliency. But before that, I want you to reflect on that opening scenario once more and think about the dream poster and goals you established when working on the activities in this chapter. Then look over the following self-reflection exercise.

My Voice

Keeping in mind the authentic you inside, answer the following:

- ▶ How can I use my dreams and goals to help me balance out what people expect from me?
- ▶ Do the expectations I hold for myself line up with the dreams I have?
- ▶ Are there adjustments I need to make to my expectations or the things I am involved in based on my inner voice?

Chapter 2

Tools . . . Not Rules

> Your parents and your teachers just want you to do your best. All the rules and such are just their ways of ensuring you're on a good path. So, hear them out, even if you don't agree. Maybe there's something in what they say that'll make a difference. —Olivia, age 17

In the last chapter, we explored the true you living deep inside and what dreams she may have. We also started to talk about goals and the map you needed to create in order to start on the journey toward your authentic self.

Now we are going to focus on some of the rules we need to abide by as we travel toward authenticity. It may seem strange talking about rules, but they are the guidelines and principals we live by in order to shape and organize our lives. In their truest sense, they aren't rigid and unyielding, but fluid and flexible. They can adjust and change as needed for a particular situation.

At least, most rules can.

But more on that in a minute. First, I want you to take a look at the following scenario.

What Would You Do?

There are a lot of rules in your house—don't get into the car with a stranger, no dating until you're 16, do what your parents and your teachers tell you to do. And on and on. You grew up knowing that you aren't supposed to break any of these rules.

One day, however, you discover that a good friend is in trouble. She's told you about some big stuff happening in her life, things involving an older boy she really likes. She's also sworn you to secrecy. Now, another rule in your household is to honor your commitments. If you promise not to share a secret, you cannot spill it. But, in this case, you're worried for your friend. Very worried.

What do you do? Tell her you are going to tell someone and risk the friendship? Try to help her solve the problem without seeking outside help? Tell your mom or dad what's going on?

Take a moment and write down what you would do to deal with this conflict between rules and secrecy.

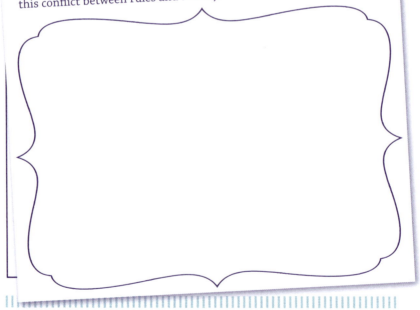

Rules, Rules, Rules

Rules—we all have them in our lives. And we all feel both comforted and stifled by them at times. Defined by Merriam-Webster as "guides toward action," rules are an everyday part of our lives. In truth, we need them in order to shape and guide communities, households, and even ourselves.

And rules can actually help you on your journey to your authentic self by helping shape how you take the trip in the first place. Knowing the rules at school and home and choosing to follow them can help you stay out of trouble and enable you to reach your final goal more quickly and easily. Understanding which rules are flexible and which rules are not—learning that type of discernment—can help you decide which path you may want to take on the journey.

One of my favorite examples of this comes from the dancer Isadora Duncan. Born in the late 1800s, Isadora is considered the creator of modern dance. She believed that dance was more than entertainment; it was a form of art and one of the best ways for humans to connect emotions to physical movement.

She did not start out with a goal of redefining the dance world. No, she was a trained ballerina who found her authentic self and then reshaped the world of dance to her vision. She was trained in the rules of classical dance and followed them until she could reshape them. She learned to discern.

As I mentioned, Isadora Duncan started with an understanding of the rules before she changed and reshaped them. This is where I'd like you to start as well. Take a moment and think about the various areas of your life that have rules—home, school, sports, art. Then complete the Rules to Live By activity. Remember, only by knowing and experiencing the rules can you learn how to discern and reshape them.

Rules to Live By

Directions: Follow the steps below to complete a series of rules for your life.

1. Using your journal or something similar, list some of the rules you are expected to follow. Think about rules at home and school and those in life.

2. Many times, your parents' expectations and a teacher's expectations match. Go through the list and find the things that are repeated. Cross out any duplicates.

3. Go through the list and write down why each item is a rule. If you are uncertain, ask your parent or teacher.

4. On a new page, make a poster listing the most common rules you are expected to follow.

5. Draw or find pictures to decorate the page with.

6. Give the poster a title.

7. Every few months, reflect back on the poster. Do you need to add to it? Or make a new poster?

8. Try to keep a current picture in mind of the rules you try to follow daily to serve as a guide toward the way you'd like to behave.

Not Rules . . . Tools

Sometimes rules can feel stifling. Maybe you're told that you have to walk a certain way or stay within the lines when coloring. This is when it's important to learn to distinguish between rules that have to do with safety and need to be followed, versus those rules that are more like guidelines or tools.

Yes, sometimes rules are really just tools for good living, generally accepted as things we need to do to live healthy lives or to follow the guiding principles of our parents and teachers.

And sometimes, you will disagree with the rules completely.

But what do you do when you disagree with the rules around you? Or when you don't understand them and want to change them in some way?

Part of growing up and becoming your own person involves discernment—learning which things you can and should challenge versus those you should not and learning how to express your views without getting yourself into trouble. It's normal for parents to have rules about your life that may be a little out of step with your maturity. The reason for this is simple—you will grow up faster than adults expect. Being able to talk with your parents and teachers about the rules that need to be changed to reflect your new maturity is an important step in finding your voice and becoming your own person. But you will get farther in this process if you can learn a little discernment first.

Take a look at the next worksheet. Using the information gathered from your Rules to Live By activity, you are going to go through the various rules you are expected to follow and decide which ones may need a little changing.

Now that you have taken a moment to really think about the rules in your life, why they are there, and which ones may need a little

The Girl Guide
Worksheet #3

Analyzing the Rules

Directions: Take a few minutes to think about what rules are in your life, why you think each may be a rule, and whether and how you could change it.

Rule	Why it's a rule	Change? (Y/N)
Brush your teeth before bed.	−To keep my teeth from getting cavities −To prevent illness	N, this is a safety rule
No e-mail or Facebook until you're 18.	−To keep me safe online	Y, I want to learn how to be online safely before I graduate and move out. So, I need this one to change (and, yes, my friends are online too!).
Rule:		
Rule:		
Rule:		
Rule:		

changing, it's time to talk with your parents. Using some of the tips in Tool #1, take a moment to speak with your parents about the rules that may be out of sync with you and your goals. See if you can find compromises. Use this as an opportunity to practice listening to your inner voice and using that as a guide.

Tool #1

Speaking Out With Finesse

- ▶ Be respectful when speaking out about rules you'd like to change or discuss.
- ▶ State your concerns clearly and with little emotion.
- ▶ Use the previous worksheet to clarify your opinions and thoughts.
- ▶ Listen to their responses without interrupting. Hear them out.
- ▶ Don't argue, but do try to keep the lines of communication open.

Taking Stock

We've spent most of the chapter talking about rules and how to discern them. We've discussed how rules guide and shape us, providing some organization for the journey inward. And we've talked about how to speak to our parents about rules we want to change.

Spend a minute thinking about the rules and your feelings about them by completing Activity #3. Are you the type to resist anything that hints of a rule? Or are you the type to follow every

Rule Follower & Rule Breaker

Directions: Follow the steps below to figure out which rules to follow and which rules to break in your life.

1. Using your journal or something similar, divide the page into two columns.

2. Title the columns Rule Follower and Rule Breaker.

3. Using the previous worksheet as a guide, list the rules you like following on one side and the rules you tend to break on the other. For example, I would list things like "Look before you cross the street" and "No texting while driving" in the Rule Follower column, and I would list "Color within the lines" and "Write in complete sentences" in the Rule Breaker column.

4. Decorate the page with things that represent you and the rules you follow or break.

5. Reflect on and change the page as you grow and change.

rule to the letter? Take a minute and listen to your inner voice and see how you authentically react to rules. For me, I am a rule follower when it comes to safety and meeting expectations of others. And I am a total rule breaker when it comes to art; I love stretching those limits.

Note to Self: Wisdom Can Come From Many Places

Nana was all of 4' 7", if that, but she was a giant in my eyes. A widow with no more than an eighth-grade education, she somehow managed to raise a daughter (my mother) all by herself. She grew fruits and vegetables in her garden and stitched all of their clothes by hand. And when her second husband died, she gave away most of her belongings so she could join us in our travels.

Nana taught me how to spin a good yarn and to turn a bad situation toward the good. As with her button tin and crocheted bookmarks, I treasure her words of wisdom even more now than when I was younger.

- *Whining doesn't do anything that singing can't do better.*
- *True beauty shines from within—you can't polish your image by bragging.*
- *Witch hazel is a magic potion. Lifesavers™ are a cure-all.*
- *Don't borrow trouble from tomorrow.*
- *Share and share alike.*
- *Stash a few goodies for the unexpected: sample-size lipsticks, for instance, and chocolate-covered cherries.*
- *It's nice to be important, but it's more important to be nice.*

> ◤ *The best mirror is an old friend.*
> ◤ *Sprinkle your pillow with lavender, and take time to smell the roses.*
>
> *Yes, they're old-school. Vintage, even. But as with all things precious, I think they stand the test of time.* —Melodye Shore

Rules, rules, rules—try as you might, the rules set by parents, teachers, and even society are going to influence you in some way. But, as you've learned, not all rules carry the same weight. This chapter was all about learning how to discern the various rules in your life.

The scenario at the start of the chapter illustrated one situation in which strict adherence to the rules may not be the best course of action. Take a moment and reflect on that scenario as you complete the self-reflection questions below.

My Voice

Keeping in mind the authentic you inside, answer the following:

◤ Are there rules that need to be broken from time to time? Which ones? How can I decide when to break them?

◤ Do I need the structure that rules give me? Or am I more comfortable when I have more freedom?

◤ What can I do if I need more freedom, but my parents/teachers need me to have more structure or rules?

Chapter 3

Starting the Journey

> *It's hard to believe in yourself. When I do poorly on a test or get into a fight with my mom, I really struggle to remember that I'm enough just as I am. That's when I try to tell myself that everyone makes mistakes, and everyone struggles. I just need to keep trying.* —Mia, age 18

With any journey, there are things we must take and actions we must do in order to start. In this chapter, we are exploring our foundation and the daily activities and habits we can engage in that will enhance our journey and give us the strength to pursue our dreams and find our inner voices. I said in the previous chapters that following your dreams and living an authentic life is one of the hardest things anyone will ever do. It requires strength, faith, patience, determination, courage, and commitment. And these attributes are all enhanced when you lead a balanced life.

In this chapter, you will explore your everyday habits and cultivate a life of balance and harmony. To start, work through the opening scenario.

What Would You Do?

You have big dreams and amazing goals. You've taken the time to picture your dreams in detail and work through some goals to lead you in the right direction. Now the unexpected has happened—your family is moving clear across country. None of your support systems will be with you, none of the teachers and programs that you had lined up to support your dreams. Nothing.

What do you do? Tell your parents you want to stay and live with a relative or friend? Suck it up and deal; after all, the promotion your dad got is a good thing? Give up on some of the goals? Adjust your goals? Put everything on hold for 5 years until you can move out?

Take a moment and write down what you would do when faced with a sudden change in plans.

Adopting a Healthy Lifestyle

As I mentioned in the opening of this chapter, following your dreams is hard work. It takes a serious amount of dedication to stay the course on the path of your dreams when life begins to throw curveballs your way. In the upcoming chapters, I will specifically talk about ways to deal with those curveballs. For now, it's important to have a strong foundation of healthy habits as you cultivate your authentic self.

Healthy habits include things like getting enough sleep, making healthy food choices, and learning to relax. It also includes building your resiliency and learning to be flexible with life's ups and downs.

Any journey can be fraught with peril. Inner journeys force us to look at the aspects of ourselves we may not like. They also force us to change—and no one really likes change. Finding the energy to cope with whatever life throws your way may be difficult when you're tired, hungry, stressed, or anxious. That is where healthy habits come into play. By making a conscious decision to make *you* a priority in your life, you are committing to a pattern of behavior that enables you to better cope with anything that comes your way. And the stronger your coping mechanisms, the better your resiliency. That leads to the attributes I mentioned earlier—strength, faith, patience, determination, courage, and commitment. Take time for yourself every day, keeping in mind the game plan in Tool #2.

As you add the components of healthy living to your daily routine, you may find it hard to fit everything you want to do into your schedule. That is where balance comes in. Different from the boundary setting I will talk about in the next section, being in balance refers to the "perfect" combination of rest, relaxation, and activity in your daily routine.

Tool #2

Taking Care of Me

▶ *Get plenty of rest*. Most teens require 8–10 hours of sleep a night. Getting enough sleep is essential to everything from proper brain functioning, to stabilizing your moods, to everything else. Developing a bedtime routine can help if you have a hard time getting to sleep at night and can include the following:

» Turn off all electronics by a specified time each night.

» Stay away from caffeine and sugar late at night.

» Practice deep breathing, meditation, or yoga before bed to settle your thoughts.

» Read or listen to relaxing music before bed.

▶ *Eat healthy foods*. This means getting a good balance of protein, carbohydrates, and fat in every meal. It also means eating plenty of fruits and vegetables and taking a good multivitamin. Commit to learning how to make good food choices and eating healthy every day.

▶ *Stay active*. Exercise is an essential part of taking care of you. Spend a part of every day being active. Dance around your room, jump rope, walk to a friend's house, play ball—all of these forms of exercise will keep you healthy, and make it easier to get to sleep at night. It will also serve as a fabulous stress reliever on the road to you.

▶ *Relax*. We live in a very busy and noisy world. Learning to relax a little every day can help rejuvenate our minds and our bodies. Try deep breathing, yoga, or prayer as a way to relax.

▶ *Playing*. Life isn't just about working toward your goals. It's easy to get too busy with school and your extra activities to remember to play. But playing is an essential part of any healthy lifestyle—as is laughing. Find a way to carve out a few minutes of playtime into your busy schedule. Include a friend, a pet, or your family—they need playtime too.

Balance isn't always easy to achieve. Some days, it is impossible to fit in exercise. And other days, there is just no time to play. This will happen. Count on it. And strive for overall balance during the week.

> *Balance . . . it is such a hard thing for me to figure out. Just when I think I have a plan to deal with all of my activities and schoolwork, something happens to throw it all out of whack. I guess I just need to keep practicing at it. But I will; I know it's important.* —Trina, age 13

The next worksheet, Creating a Life of Balance, can help you figure out how you spend your time and where you may need to prioritize things differently in order to achieve better balance. This worksheet is a quick way to determine what areas you may need to focus on and incorporate more into your life. As a bonus activity, keep track of the time you spend in each area. Are you surprised by the results?

Healthy Boundaries

Another aspect of healthy living and the development of a good foundation from which to start your journey inward involves the development of healthy boundaries, both in terms of the boundaries you set with others and the way you act. A boundary is something that sets a limit. In this conversation, it refers to understanding the limits between you and another person or activity.

The first boundary I want to discuss has to do with what you can and cannot control in your life. You can control you. But you

Worksheet #4: Creating a Life of Balance

Directions: Take a few minutes to answer the questions below and determine what your priorities are. Be sure to answer the questions at the end.

1. **Rest**
   — Do I get at least 6 hours of sleep every night?
   — Am I tired throughout the day?
   — Do I use the weekends to "catch up" on sleeping?
   — Is getting enough rest a priority for me?

2. **Eating Healthy**
   — Do I know how to construct a healthy and well-balanced meal?
   — Do I have a variety of food options available to me in my home?
   — Do I take vitamins daily?
   — If I don't have access to healthy food at home, do I utilize the food options at school and make this a priority?

3. **Exercise**
   — Do I make getting some form of physical exercise each day a priority?
   — Am I involved in some sort of sport? How often?
   — Do I feel "off" when I do not exercise?
   — Is finding time for physical activities a priority for me?

4. **Relaxation**
   — Do I think relaxing is important to my overall health?
   — Do I find myself "on edge" or anxious throughout the day?
   — Do I try to meditate, pray, or do yoga at least twice a week?
   — Do I have planned moments of silence during my day?

5. **Playtime**
   — Do I find time to play every day? My playtime activities include . . .
   — Do I think playing is as important as doing my homework and other activities?
   — Do I prefer playing alone to playing with a friend or a pet?
   — I think playing is important because . . .

Worksheet #4 Continued

Once you are finished, reflect on your answers. Where do you place your priorities? Which items are you good at including? Which items need more of your attention? Take a moment to write down your thoughts on these aspects of healthy living and creating some balance in your life.

can't control someone else, no matter how much you try. Sure, you can attempt to manipulate a situation to a specific outcome. But ultimately, you aren't in control of that situation—only your reaction to the situation and your thoughts about it.

Although you may not have control over what other people do in your life, you do have 100% control over yourself and your thoughts. This is a hard fact to accept for many. In fact, you may have had a strong reaction when reading this, believing you can't really control your thoughts. But you can. And you do. Every day. All of the self-talk and all of the ways you listen and respond to that self talk *is* taking control of it.

Now, I know it's hard to acknowledge responsibility for your actions and beliefs. But the truth is, no one can tell you what to think and feel. Likewise, you can't make someone else feel or act a certain way. You only have control over you.

The following activity is designed to help you remember that you control you. And only you. Nothing else. It is an important boundary to remember when you interact with the world.

Although you have no control over others, your actions can influence another's actions. When you are mean to someone, that person will likely be mean to you. When you are generous, you will often receive generosity in return. Setting appropriate boundaries with others and living by the "Golden Rule" of treating others as you would like to be treated is a great way to enhance your commitment to living healthy and help you along the path toward yourself. Clear boundaries help ensure that everyone stays true to themselves, without negatively influencing others. Clear boundaries also help us stay on the path toward our dreams by enabling us to discern the things we can change and influence from the things we cannot.

Activity #4

My Boundaries

Directions: Using the steps below, discover what your healthy boundaries should be and what you can and can't control.

1. Using a fresh page in your journal or a blank piece of paper, draw a large circle in the center of the page. Try to fill up at least half of the page with your circle.

2. In the center of the circle, write your name (or draw a picture of yourself). Using colored pencils or pictures, fill the circle with things that represent your thoughts, actions, and beliefs. Put only the things that represent your thoughts, actions, and beliefs inside the circle. These are the things in your life you can control—just your thoughts, actions, and beliefs.

3. Around the outside of the circle, list all of the things you can't control, such as other people's actions, the weather, what your parents do or think, and so on.

4. Decorate the outside of the circle with pictures to represent those things you cannot control.

5. Keep the picture some place handy and refer to it every time you find yourself trying to control another person or situation or any time you are upset about something.

Reaching Your Potential

You've spent a lot of time over the past three chapters clarifying your dreams, figuring out who you are right now and where you want to go, setting goals, discerning life's rules, and setting boundaries. There is one more concept I want to introduce you to before we go deeper into this journey.

Resiliency.

As I mentioned in the introduction to this part of the book, resiliency refers to the ability to bounce back after a setback or adjust to change. There are several attributes that help someone become more resilient. These include having a sense of connectedness to others, believing in yourself and your problem-solving abilities, and understanding *who* you are as an emotional being. You will explore each of these areas in a lot of detail in the upcoming chapters. For now, I want you to think of resiliency as the driving force that will help you reach the dreams you set forth in Chapter 1, discern and take control of the rules you analyzed in Chapter 2, and enabled you to set clear boundaries in this chapter.

As you prepare to actually start your journey inward and go deeper into your strengths and areas in need of attention, take a moment to do the next activity, The Real Me. You are an amazing young woman just as you are. Realizing your potential means enhancing the you that already exists and bringing her to the forefront.

Activity #5 — The Real Me

Directions: Follow the steps below to help find the real you.

1. Go back to the Who Am I? worksheet from Chapter 1. Using that as a springboard, make a list of the character traits that define you.

2. Next, make another list of the positive adjectives people have used to describe you—think of the things said by friends, family, teachers, and others.

3. Now, list your goals and dreams for the future. Refer to your dream poster if you need to.

4. Make a list of the things you like to do and how you like to spend your time.

5. After making your lists, draw or find pictures that illustrate the things from your list. Make a collage in the journal or on a separate card for you to look back on anytime you forget the truth about you. Be creative with this. You can make the collage in the shape of a person, an object, or anything else that represents you. You could also decorate an old CD or DVD case, using the front cover to showcase your collage and the back cover to share the lists you made in steps 2-4. Set the case on a shelf slightly open so it will stand upright, and you'll have a frequent reminder of the real you!

6. Take this to the next level by creating a video collage or Pinterest boards that represent all of the areas of your life.

Note to Self:
Plan Ahead or Go Behind

Proper planning can prevent a lot of heartache down the road. So, don't leap ahead without first thinking about what you need for life's little journeys. —Maria Tumilty

And now the journey begins. It will be one of the most exciting journeys you will ever take. And one of the hardest. But you have prepared yourself for the tasks that lay ahead. Now, you just need to start down the path.

Earlier, you wrote down what you would do if faced with a major roadblock to your dreams. I want you to think about that scenario and all of the things you've learned about setting boundaries and practicing healthy habits. Would any of that have helped you navigate through that difficult scenario differently?

Take a moment to reflect on the exercise below before beginning the next section.

My Voice

Keeping in mind the authentic you inside, answer the following:

- What are some things I can do to stay on the path toward my dreams when life throws me a curveball?
- What attributes of resiliency do I currently think I have?
- How will remembering the boundary exercises and the healthy living tips help me stay on track?
- Am I ready for the journey? Why or why not?

Part II

It's All About Connections

Human beings are social by nature. We need the connections we make with friends and adults to give us the support we need to face some of life's adversities. This doesn't mean we have to surround ourselves with tons of friends or have a "perfect" family, whatever that means, in order to feel support. Not at all. All we really need is to believe that we have a network of people in our lives who understand us and who we can rely on.

Building connections and deriving support from those connections involves developing good social skills so that you feel comfortable around others, having tolerance to different points of view, and knowing how to lean on others when things get difficult. Some of these skills you may already have, and some may really challenge you. But you need to fine-tune these skills as you enter adolescence and the nature of your relationships change and grow.

As we begin this part of your journey toward developing good social skills and cultivating a network of support, I think it's important for you to take stock of where you currently stand in this regard. Answer the five true/false questions in the quiz now, and come back after reading through the section and completing some of the tasks to see how your perspective may have changed.

Quiz #2

Thinking About My Support System

1. I have friends and family I can trust with my secrets.

   ☐ True ☐ False

2. When things are hard, I have people in my life I can turn to for support.

   ☐ True ☐ False

3. I feel comfortable asking for help from teachers, family members, or friends.

   ☐ True ☐ False

4. It is okay to have disagreements with the friends in my social group.

   ☐ True ☐ False

5. I think it's important for people to be able to express their own points of view, and I like to express my point of view, even when it is different from my friends.

   ☐ True ☐ False

Chapter 4

The Social Game

> *Never stop being you because you are trying to "fit in" with some group. You'll just make yourself miserable! —Madison, age 15*

Now that you have started the journey toward your authentic self, it's time to focus on the first leg of the journey—social connections. Human beings are social creatures by nature. As social organisms, one of our most basic needs is to feel like we belong, like we can and do relate to others within a social context. It is a huge part of who we are.

But what happens when you can't connect for one reason or another? What happens when you don't feel comfortable around others, or when you feel like people don't understand you?

This chapter explores the various aspects of social relatedness and how to draw comfort from others in a healthy way, as well as why this is a critical skill. But first, it's time to test your social savvy in the following scenario.

What Would You Do?

You don't consider yourself a very sociable person. In fact, if it was up to you, you'd keep to yourself or spend any free time reading, as opposed to hanging out with other kids. Your parents think that you struggle with making friends. But from your perspective, you just aren't comfortable around people. They make you feel "prickly" inside and create feelings of anxiety whenever you have to spend long periods of time in social situations.

Now, your parents have asked you—no, told you—to get involved in more activities, an idea that makes you squirm.

What do you do? Ignore your parents' request? Choose something, anything, and then drop out? Decide your parents are right and try to get more involved? Talk with your parents about your feelings and try to get them to back off?

Take a moment and write down what you would do to navigate through this scenario.

Comfort With Many and With a Few

As I mentioned earlier, not everyone has the same level of comfort with other people. Some of you may need social connections as much as you need air, thriving on the social scene as a source of energy and renewal. Others of you may view social situations as horrible moments you have to endure. And many of you fall somewhere in between.

In truth, all of us tend toward one extreme or the other. The easiest way to figure out which is true for you is to first look at how you naturally renew your emotional self. In other words, are you *energized* or *drained* by extended periods around other people?

If social connections are energizing to you, you may find that you need to talk with friends or adults in order to feel rejuvenated. You may want to retell your day, talk through your problems out loud, and hang out with others just to relax. In fact, you may feel more anxious or stressed when you are alone.

For those of you who need solitude in order to emotionally renew, you may tend to shy away from too many social contacts. You may get cranky when you are around people for too long. In fact, you will likely prefer to be alone, reading a book or writing in a journal instead of talking through your problems with others.

It's important to know which of the two extremes is more representative of you. This information can help you better determine when to insert yourself into a social situation and when it may be best to simply be alone. Complete the short worksheet that follows to help you determine whether you are more extroverted, meaning you often renew through social contact, or introverted, meaning you renew through solitude.

The Girl Guide

Worksheet #5: How I Recharge

Directions: Take a few minutes to answer the questions below to determine if you need social isolation in order to truly renew or if you thrive off of social connections. At the end, reflect on your answers.

- ▶ Your mom asks you about your day the second you get in the car after a very busy day. Do you:
  - ☐ Answer briefly and close your eyes, desperate for a little quiet?
  - ☐ Chat with her openly about every little detail about the day? _____
  - ☐ Other: _____

- ▶ You are assigned to a group for a project at school. Do you:
  - ☐ Ask the teacher if you can do the project alone? You'll do it better by yourself.
  - ☐ Get excited and talk with everyone in the group?
  - ☐ Other :_____

- ▶ You are new to your school. Do you:
  - ☐ Watch and hang back a bit, just to understand the social dynamics?
  - ☐ Jump in and make friends? _____
  - ☐ Other: _____

- ▶ When you are alone after a busy day, would you rather:
  - ☐ Read a book or listen to music alone in your room?
  - ☐ Sit and talk with your mom or sibling or hang out with a friend?
  - ☐ Other: _____

»

Worksheet #5 Continued

Look over your answers. If you said that you mostly like to go it alone, you are more introverted. If social connections are the key to your renewal, you are more likely an extrovert. Understanding which dynamic is true for you can help you plan for opportunities to recharge. What are some ways you can renew?

After the worksheet is complete, take a moment to think about some of the important people in your life. Just as you tend more toward introversion or extroversion, so do they. Knowing what is true for them can help you know how to respect their needs as well.

Social Savvy

Part of developing strong social connections and deriving comfort from those relationships is developing a little social savvy. Before we jump into what that means, I want you to complete the following worksheet, Social Savvy Smarts, and identify both your strengths and difficulties in the social arena.

Now that you have a clearer picture of your particular social skills development, take a moment and identify your areas of strength and areas you need to improve. What can you do to develop some of your weaker skills? Complete Activity #6 and make a game plan of how you will develop some of your social skills.

When Comfort Can't Be Found

As I mentioned at the start of the chapter, human beings are social organisms requiring social connections in order to thrive. Comfort within these connections can make a big difference on the road to your authentic self. But sometimes, finding this comfort is a challenge.

Feeling secure in social situations is a factor of both your temperament and your individual social skills development. Although you won't change how you're hard-wired (extroverted or introverted), your ability to develop your social skills and your ability to deal with social anxiety will most certainly impact your depth of

The Girl Guide
Worksheet #6

Social Savvy Smarts

Directions: Fill in the following chart to note which social skills you agree and disagree with.

Skill	I agree	I disagree
I say "please" and "thank you."		
I take turns in a conversation.		
I let other people lead a conversation from time to time.		
I am comfortable starting a new conversation.		
In class, I am comfortable working in a group.		
At a party, I am comfortable meeting new people.		
When I disagree with a friend or teacher, I can calmly express my point of view.		
Arguments do not last long with my friends.		
I understand the "social rules" with my friends.		
When my friends and I argue, I am usually the one to make things better.		

Social Diva 101

Directions: Follow the steps below to help you find your social savvy.

1. Using the Social Savvy Smarts worksheet as a guide, pick 5-10 rules you think are important in terms of making and keeping friends.

2. On a card or in your journal, write down your social rules.

3. Decorate your list with things that remind you of each rule.

4. Read the list anytime you feel a little awkward in social situations. You may want to add the list to the Notes section of your phone so it's handy when you don't know what to do about a social challenge.

comfort with others—and ultimately, your ability to thrive along your personal self-discovery journey.

For some of you, the level of discomfort with others is extreme, preventing you from feeling okay in most social situations. Keeping in mind some of the techniques you learned in the previous chapters, like the My Boundaries activity, read through the Social Anxiety Busters tool below. Take a few minutes in your journal to reflect on ways that this tool can help you conquer your social discomfort and learn to derive more strength from your social connections.

Tool #3

Social Anxiety Busters

- Focus on healthy living including appropriate eating, sleeping, and exercise routines.
- Spend time relaxing every day.
- Pay attention to how you talk to yourself. Positive self-talk will help combat any social anxiety.
- Be mindful and realistic in your point of view.
- If you find yourself particularly stressed over a specific event, mentally rehearse the event, focusing on successfully completing the activity.

Note to Self: Choose to Be a Source of Positive Change

Life can be hard and people can be cruel. But the world can also be profoundly beautiful. And people can astound you with their capacity for kindness. Always be aware of the darkness and danger, but live for the wonder that each day brings. Treat people the way you would like to be treated and see the good in all situations. Choose to be a source of positive change in the world. —Elle Horne

Feeling comfortable around other people isn't something that comes easily for everyone. But whether you're a social butterfly or social misfit, believing that there are people in your corner to support you and feeling comfortable enough to accept their help can make a huge difference in your ability to face life's challenges. Additionally, seeing yourself as competent in social domains can help give you the confidence you need as you search for your authentic self.

As the earlier scenario may suggest, lots of things impact your comfort with other people including your temperament, overall social savvy, and resources to combat anxiety. Think about the opening scenario and the things you have learned in this chapter as you reflect on and answer the questions that follow.

My Voice

Keeping in mind the authentic you inside, answer the following:

- Am I comfortable around others? Why or why not?
- Think of a time when you have felt comfortable with others. What was something good that came out of the experience? Were you helped in some way?
- Think of your friends and their temperaments. Does knowing more about their comfort help you in any way? How?

Chapter 5

Team Me

> *I really need to embrace who I am instead of putting myself down because I don't really fit in.* —Samantha, age 14

Feeling comfortable with others is only one part of strengthening your social connectedness. Trusting that people will be there to support you through thick and thin, as well as trusting that others will not negatively judge you or treat you in a disingenuous way also have the power to impact your ability to connect with others.

As we begin to go deeper and explore the different ways that the adults and friends in your life can support Team Me, I want to start by examining the following scenario related to trust.

What Would You Do?

Something is wrong with Katie! Friends since you were both in kindergarten, Katie isn't acting much like a friend now that you're in eighth grade. She is nice when your mom carpools you both to gymnastics, but shuns you as soon as your mom drives off. At school, she acts as if she doesn't know you. Worse, she acts like you are the worst thing on campus. You've tried to talk with her about how you feel, but every time you bring it up she says you're imagining things.

Recently, Katie started ignoring you during carpool, too, talking on the phone or putting in her earbuds as soon as she gets in the car. You are ready to call it quits to the friendship, but you're worried that there isn't anyone else who knows you as well as she does. You don't make friends easily, and the thought of putting yourself out there is enough to make you ill.

What do you do? Change who *you* are to try to fit in with Katie? Tell your parents in the hopes that they can fix whatever is wrong? Risk rejection to make new friends? Just deal with your problems alone—who needs friends anyway?

Take a moment and write down what you would do.

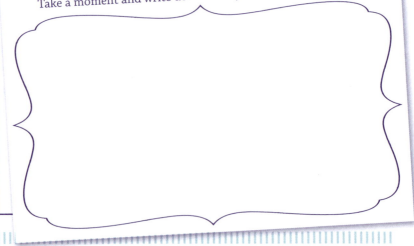

Building a Network of Support

I mentioned in the last chapter that human beings are social organisms, predisposed to develop relationships. We need a sense of community in order to thrive—people that we believe understand us and will support us through the difficult times.

Sadly, not every girl feels a strong sense of support in her daily life. Sometimes this happens as a result of events that tear apart the family and home environment. Sometimes this happens due to barriers involving medical conditions of one form or another. And sometimes this happens because you just don't *see* the support around you, even when it is there.

> My aunt died last year. She was a really important person to me. After I lost her, I felt like I had no one who really understood me. No one I could lean on. It wasn't until my mom made me make a list of the people in my life that I felt close to that I realized that I still had a good support system. —Lina, age 17

In order for you to feel supported and to benefit from that support, you first need to recognize all of the resources you have. Home, school, church, sports—these are all venues that can provide connections and support. Take a moment to work through Worksheet #7 and see how many people you can identify as sources of possible support in your life.

Once you've gone through the worksheet and isolated the people who can serve as your support system, it's time to add it to your journal. Follow the activity My Circle of Support and create a picture that can be a reminder of everyone who makes up Team Me.

Worksheet #7

My Support System

Directions: Take a few minutes to use the guidelines below to determine what makes up your support system.

1. List all of the places you spend time during the week, including school, church, and family time.

   a. _____

   b. _____

   c. _____

   d. _____

   e. _____

   f. _____

2. For each place, list as many people as you can that you feel safe with, people who understand and support you.

3. Reread the list, adding and subtracting people as you grow and change.

4. Use the list to assist you with the next activity.

My Circle of Support

Directions: Follow the steps below to create a circle of supportive individuals in your life.

1. Write the word "Me" in the center of the circle. Fill in each line with the name of someone who is part of "Team Me"—people you know you can turn to if you need support or guidance. Pull from the list in the previous worksheet for help if you need it.

2. Revisit and adjust the circle of support as needed.

The journey toward your inner self can often feel like a lonely endeavor. Knowing that you have supporters on the journey can make the difference between staying the course and abandoning your efforts. On those hard days—and yes, there will be some very difficult moments on the path toward your authentic self—pull out your journal and reflect on your Circle of Support. These are your cheerleaders, your fangirls, your peeps. These are the people who will have your back and root for you, no matter what.

Trust Yourself

Sometimes your support system lets you down. They may even abandon you as you become more of your authentic self and less the person they thought they knew. When this happens, it may be difficult for you to trust new friends or supporters. It may even be difficult for you to trust yourself. This reaction is completely understandable.

And not entirely correct.

When friendships change and you no longer have the support you once thought you had, it's important to regroup and remember the truth of what you have. Odds are your friends haven't really left. And if they have, there's a good chance you can find new friends. And when in doubt, you can rely on your own internal strengths to get you through. The key is remembering that you have options—many options—including learning to appreciate yourself and everything that means.

In the first chapters, you took some time to discover the various aspects of you. Go back and read your journal entries. Appreciate who you are at your core, not who you think others want you to be. When you can accept yourself and your friends for who they are, and when you are willing to trust that who you are is enough, that is when you truly begin to connect and when you strengthen and develop that aspect of resiliency.

Accepting Your Friends, Warts and All

- ▸ Think about your friends and some of their habits that frustrate you.
- ▸ Focus on one behavior that is frustrating to you, not the person.
- ▸ Write down the behavior that is concerning.
- ▸ Write down a few reasons why that friend may engage in those behaviors.
- ▸ Decide if the behavior is a big deal, something you can't get past, or a little annoyance. If it is a big deal, talk with your friend to work it out. If it is a little annoyance, consider just letting it go.

Being Enough

Trusting yourself and others requires more than acceptance. It requires the inner belief that you and your friends are enough just as you are. This is a very difficult concept for most people to grasp.

I want to share a little story with you about a girl named Tina I once knew; an awkward and shy girl, Tina struggled with making social connections. There were lots of reasons for this, but mostly it just came down to a lack of trust that she was enough as she was. A lack of acceptance of herself.

Tina spent a lot of her middle school years trying to fit in with others, changing her interests, dressing and acting differently. None of it worked. No matter how hard she tried to be someone other than who she was, her larger-than-life personality always managed to give herself away and reveal her authentic self, whether she wanted that or not.

It took Tina more than 20 years to finally grow into that large personality. And even as an adult, she continued to struggle with her sense of self, still retreating into the same question that plagued her as a child: "Am I enough?"

I want to take a minute to tell Tina, and you, that you are enough as you are right now. Period. Could you achieve more, do more, be more? Sure. But that isn't the question, is it? The question was, are you enough? To that I say a resounding YES.

There is a great book for babies and toddlers entitled *On the Day That You Were Born* by Debra Frasier. In it, the author explains the basics of gravity, the tides, the moon, and other worldly phenomena as she welcomes humanity to the planet. It is a poignant little book and illustrates the "You're enough" message with profound beauty.

Take a moment and reflect on the concept of being enough as you are. Think about how your friends are enough right now too. Then complete the next activity and make a few friendship cards for your friends. Don't forget to make one for the most important friend you will ever have—you!

"We Are Enough" Friendship Cards

Directions: Using the directions below, create a series of cards that reflect your relationships.

1. In your journal, make a list of your friends.

2. For each friend, make two lists: one of the things she (or he!) likes to do, another of the reasons you think she is a good friend.

3. For each friend, make a separate page in your journal for or write on a card phrases that express both her interests and the reasons she is a good friend.

4. Add photos or drawings of you and your friends to each page or card.

5. Refer back to the pages/cards any time things feel a little strained with a friend. You may even turn the cards into real greeting cards and stick them in your friend's locker or backpack as a surprise to let her know how awesome you think she is!

6. To take this activity further, make movies of your friends using the pictures and music that represents your friendship. Watch the movies anytime you need to remember all of the reasons you are friends.

Note to Self: Respect Yourself

Respect yourself first and foremost. It's easy to say, but hard to do. You are wonderful, unique, and beautiful in ways you can't even imagine. Never let anyone tell you different, but at the same time don't forget to remain humble and treat others with kindness. Stand up for yourself; don't wait for others to do it.
—Heather McCorkle

Taking time to acknowledge and develop your support system is one of the most valuable things you can do along the journey inward. Begin with reviewing the My Support System worksheet and My Circle of Support activity. Revisit the friendship cards. And take time to remember that you have everything you need with you, right now. The trick is getting in touch with that inner voice enough to hear it and believing that you are enough right now as you are. As you grow and strengthen these attributes, your ability to connect to others and derive support will also strengthen.

The next chapter focuses on tolerance and respect. Before we proceed, take a moment and reflect on the earlier scenarios and the various activities throughout the chapter as you complete the self-reflection questions that follow.

My Voice

Keeping in mind the authentic you inside, answer the following:

▶ Name someone you can trust completely. What has this person done that tells you that he or she is trustworthy?

▶ How hard was it for you to develop a circle of support? Do you find it difficult to rely on others? Why or why not?

▶ I spoke a lot about being "enough" as you are. How did you feel when you first read the phrase? Was it hard to accept that truth about yourself? Why or why not?

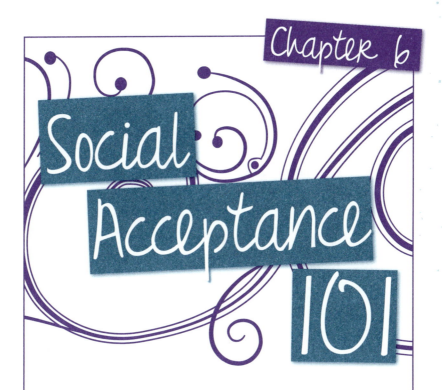

Chapter 6

Social Acceptance 101

> Never put people in a box, or let yourself be put in a box. You are whoever you'd like to be. Don't settle for less. —Kaitlyn, age 17

The last aspect of social connectedness I want to discuss relates to respect and tolerance. Building on the acceptance concepts from the previous chapter, respect and tolerance relate to how you view the world and how you want other people to view you.

Take a look at the next scenario as you think about your definitions of respect and tolerance. Then decide, what would you do?

What Would You Do?

You have a lot of friends from many different backgrounds and personality types at school. At lunch, two of your friends tell you that they don't like another member of the group. In fact, they put a lot of pressure on you to ditch the friend, threatening to leave if you don't tell your friend to find a different group to have lunch with. You don't want to hurt your friend, but you don't want to lose your other friends either.

What do you do? Tell your friends to get over themselves? Tell the other friend you'll hang out with her at a different time? Nothing?

Take a moment and write down what you would do to navigate through this sticky situation.

Needs and Wants

One of the cornerstones of building connections relates to your tolerance for other people and your willingness to try to see things from their perspective. We live in a big world with people of differing backgrounds and points of view. And each and every person, including you, has a right to her unique perspective. Recognizing and accepting others' needs can be very difficult, especially if their needs and wants differ or are in contradiction to your own.

So what do you do? How do you let someone else have her own point of view and opinion when it is so different from your own? Is her perspective wrong simply because it is different? Do her needs outweigh yours somehow?

The answer you give to these questions may strongly influence your ability to connect with others and the path your inward journey takes.

In truth, no one person's needs supersede the needs of another. The trick is figuring out how to balance another person's needs with your own. The first step is in distinguishing a true need from a want.

A need is something you cannot live without, whereas a want is something you desire. Granted, you may really, really desire something like earning a good grade on a test or being part of a certain profession. But those are not needs; you don't require them in order to live.

No matter how strong a want, it never supersedes someone's needs.

Figuring out how to balance your needs with the needs of others can be tough. It takes a lot of practice in order to recognize the difference between a need and a want. And it can be very difficult to give up your wants in favor of someone else's needs. Take a moment and complete the Needs vs. Wants worksheet. Practice telling the difference between the two, and in no time you'll learn how to get your needs met while still respecting the needs of others.

Tolerant Is as Tolerant Does

When you begin recognizing other people's needs, you may find that you naturally become more tolerant and respectful of other people in general. And that is a huge step in a positive direction toward establishing healthy relationships that can help you thrive.

Tolerance not only relates to your tolerance of others, however. In terms of your journey inward and building strong relationships, tolerance also refers to your belief that you can express your ideas safely, especially when they differ from another person's. It's about mutual tolerance, and it is best achieved through the establishment of a respectful environment.

But how do you create a respectful setting? How do you ensure that you are respected?

Respect begins with many of the things we've already discussed—having appropriate boundaries, distinguishing between wants and needs, and having trust and support. It also involves perspective taking—understanding that there are many points of view to any situation. Cultivating the flexibility necessary to see the world from many points of view can lead to an understanding and tolerance of others, as well as cultivating increased respect. Take a moment to complete the Fresh Perspectives activity to help you build this flexibility.

The Girl Guide

Worksheet #8 · Needs vs. Wants

Directions: Go through and list as many items or events as you can think of related to home and school. These are things you may want and/or need. Then go through and indicate if it is a need or a want and why. Any time something comes up that you think you need, add it to the list and really think about whether or not it is a need or a want.

Event or Item	Need	Want
Get a Facebook account.	My teachers use Facebook as a way to communicate information about my extracurricular activities.	

Fresh Perspectives

Directions: The following list will give you some activities you can try in order to develop the habit of taking a new perspective from time to time.

1. The next time you read a story, pretend you are one of the characters and write a few sentences about what it is like to be that character.

2. Grab a camera or your journal and take a picture of a flower from three perspectives—far away, normal, and extremely close up. What did you notice about the different perspectives?

3. Draw three pictures of your room from three different perspectives. What did you learn about each point of view?

4. Role-play an argument with a friend. Then switch characters. Did your perspective of the argument change in any way?

> *I never understand why people struggle to accept each other. The way I see if, we are all in this together, right? We have a lot more in common that we may think.* —Raeleen, age 12

Learning to view the world from many different points of view will broaden your own view and allow you to go deeper as you search for your authentic and unique place in the world. And it will help you respect others.

Respect is defined by Merriam-Webster as the "act of giving attention or holding in high regard." In other words, taking the time to consider another person and her needs. Sounds like everything we've been talking about, right? Respect leads to trust. And trust builds tolerance. All of it leads to stronger connections and better resiliency. It also fosters authenticity.

Complete the next worksheet, Thinking About Respect, and test out your respect know-how.

Friendship Drama

Respect and tolerance can go a long way to ward off some of the typical drama associated with middle and high school. But being a good problem solver can also come in handy when it comes to friendships. Making and maintaining friends requires that we are both aware of our own ideas and behaviors and respectful of our friends' ideas and behaviors. This can be challenging, especially if you have not taken the time to understand yourself deeply.

Friends have the uncanny ability to be a mirror for us, reflecting back some of the more uncomfortable aspects of ourselves. This can lead to feelings of guilt, shame, and even anger. You may

The Girl Guide

Directions: Take a moment and read over the questions below. For each one, choose the answer that best reflects what you would do, not what you think *should* be done. We'll reflect on your answers at the end of the exercise.

Scenario #1: Your friend has just given a presentation in class in which you noticed a lot of mistakes regarding the information she has presented. Do you:

- a. Point out the mistakes during the presentation?
- b. Talk to your friend afterward and point out the mistakes?
- c. Let the teacher handle it. It really isn't your place to correct your classmate, even if she is your friend.
- d. Other: _____

Scenario #2: Your friend is having a hard day and is crying. Do you:

- a. Ignore her completely and walk away?
- b. Ask her what's wrong and insist on helping her settle down?
- c. Ask her what's wrong, but step away if she asks you to give her some space?
- d. Other: _____

Scenario #3: Your friend just got a new outfit and wore it to school—and it is horrible! Do you:

- a. Tell her it's hideous?
- b. Tell her you don't like it, but it looks okay on her?
- c. Don't say anything unless she asks, and then ask her if she likes it.
- d. Other: _____

Scenario #4: Your friend walks into the last period of the day totally upset. A mutual friend completely bashed her during lunch. Do you:

- a. Tell her to just ignore it, it'll blow over eventually?
- b. Help her plot her revenge?
- c. Try to make her feel better without getting involved?
- d. Other: _____

Take a moment to look over your answers. Do you behave in a way that promotes respect? Are there things you need to work on?

react by lashing out at your friends for silly reasons, not recognizing that you aren't really mad at them per se, just embarrassed or ashamed about the things their behavior is reflecting back in you.

One way to combat this type of situation is to remember the My Boundaries activity from Chapter 3. You may not be able to control how your friends act, but you can certainly control your response. The next time you feel angry and frustrated toward a friend, take a minute to ask yourself why. Is she reflecting back something that bothers you? Are you mad at her or embarrassed at yourself? Taking a few moments to take stock will go a long way to preventing unnecessary drama and taking responsibility for your own actions.

Problems and disagreements are bound to happen in relationships. It's normal. How you deal with the problem is what matters. Do you play the blame game and focus on who is right or wrong in the situation? Or do you focus on solving the problem itself? Generally speaking, you can't be right and solve problems at the same time.

When you engage in blaming behavior, you aren't focusing on problem solving. Nor are you communicating that you care about the relationship. But when you decide that it doesn't matter who is at fault, when you just focus on moving forward, that is when everything shifts. Now, you are in a position to hear the concerns your friend has, compromise solutions to the problem, and move in a positive direction. Focusing on solutions requires both parties to be willing to be a little wrong in order to move forward. It also requires abandoning blame in order to focus on problems within the relationship itself and strategizing solutions. This may mean that you will have to let go of the things that hurt you, shift your thinking, and focus on preventing future problems.

Being a problem solver also taps into perspective taking. As I mentioned before, this can be difficult. Think of it like a kaleidoscope—sometimes all you need to do to figure out a problem is turn the knob a bit and view things from a new angle.

Take a minute and reflect on your problem solving know-how. Then complete Activity #10 to remind yourself to focus on solutions.

Note to Self: Ask for Help and Give Help

Life is hard. It just is. And it's okay to admit that and ask for help when you need it. Know yourself. Trust yourself. And reach out to others, getting to know and trust them. We are all part of a larger community.
—Abby Mohaupt

Being Solution Focused

Directions: Use the steps below to help you find solutions to your problems.

1. On a card or in your journal, write down the problem you are facing.

2. Underneath the problem, begin to brainstorm every possible solution you can think of. Do not edit the list.

3. Every time you catch yourself saying "I don't know" inside, ask yourself this question: "If I did know, what would I say?", then begin to write what your next thoughts are.

4. Evaluate your potential solutions and pick three that could work to solve the problem.

5. Pick a solution and implement it.

6. Remain flexible—if the solution you picked doesn't solve the problem, try another one.

7. Be willing to ask for help if you need it.

We've talked a lot about acceptance, tolerance, and being authentic in this chapter. As girls, you face a lot of pressure from peers and society to conform to a particular way of acting. And when you don't, when you fail to be ladylike or live up to some stereotype of what that means, you may lose a little of the progress you have made toward your authentic self. But remember this—you are the only one who gets to decide what is authentic for you and what is not. I don't decide that, and neither does anyone else. Only you.

It's a big responsibility, being in charge of yourself. And yes, you will be influenced by those around you, including your parents and friends. But ultimately it is you who will decide what is right and what is wrong. You will determine your future, whether you mean to or not. And you will decide who you are on the inside.

So how will you define your life? Will you learn to embrace others' differences and unique qualities and let that strengthen both you and your relationships? Will you be gentle to yourself and your friends? Will you trust that you have a strong support system?

It is certainly harder to do these things. It takes commitment to walk the path of acceptance—commitment to defend those with no voice.

As I stated when you started this journey, the path to one's unique self is a hard one. And you will need passion and strength to venture out in search of your true self. But the end result will be worth it as you discover just how amazing you can be!

The next section will focus on the development of a positive outlook and attitude. But before we leave the conversation about relationships, take a moment to consider the self-reflection questions that follow.

My Voice

Keeping in mind the authentic you inside, answer the following:

- ► Are you calm when you disagree with others? How do you show your disagreement?
- ► How do you define "fair"? Do you think most people are fair most of the time? Why or why not?
- ► What is the hardest part of being tolerant for you? Why?
- ► Do you consider yourself an accepting person? Why or why not?

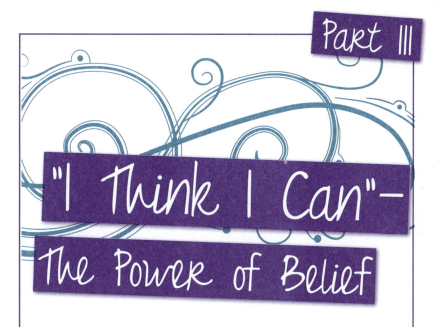

Part III

"I Think I Can"– The Power of Belief

We've all heard about the power of thinking positive. Our teachers and parents tell us all the time. But what does that really mean, and why does it work?

Positive thinking refers to your individual belief that you can master your environment and achieve your goals. In other words, it means that you believe that there is a connection between working hard, thinking positive, and achieving your goals.

In the following chapters, you will learn how having a positive outlook, developing strong problem-solving skills, and being able to learn from your mistakes can all lead to achieving your goals and dreams.

As with the other sections, the first place to start is with a little quiz to help you determine what you think about goal setting and positive thinking. Take the five-question quiz, and come back after you've read the chapters to see if anything has changed.

The Girl Guide

Quiz #3

The Power of Belief

1. I see the bright side of situations most of the time.
   - ☐ True   ☐ False

2. When I am faced with a problem, I can usually figure out a way to solve it.
   - ☐ True   ☐ False

3. Things are always better than they appear.
   - ☐ True   ☐ False

4. If the first solution to a problem doesn't work, I can always find another solution.
   - ☐ True   ☐ False

5. It's hard for me to listen to my parents or my teachers when they are telling me that I made a mistake.
   - ☐ True   ☐ False

Retake the quiz whenever you're feeling a little off track. Then revisit the activities to get yourself back on the path toward your goals and dreams.

Chapter 7

The Confidence Key

> *Stand up for what you believe in, even when it means you are standing alone. —Nira, age 16*

The first two sections of this book dealt with exploring your dreams, establishing goals, and building connections. Next, it's time to focus on developing a healthy and positive outlook on life, as well as the habits needed to complete the journey toward your unique self. And it all starts with developing a healthy confidence in your abilities, one that is realistic and positively oriented.

As you read over the next scenario, think about your own sense of confidence and begin to listen to the messages you give yourself regarding your abilities. That little voice inside has a lot more influence on your performance than you may realize.

What Would You Do?

You have always been a strong athlete. Whether it's soccer or softball, you excel in sports and you always have. So it's no surprise that you made the varsity soccer team as a freshman. There's only one problem—your grades are horrible. As much as you excel in sports, you struggle in class. And now your grades endanger your ability to play competitive sports at school. Your mom has offered to get a tutor, but the idea of spending *more* time working on your studies, something you hate, is enough to make you physically ill.

What do you do? Give up your position on the team? Try the tutor and see if it will work? Just try harder on your own? Give up completely? Pretend the problem will go away and just stay focused on playing soccer?

Take a moment and write down what you would do to deal with this difficult situation.

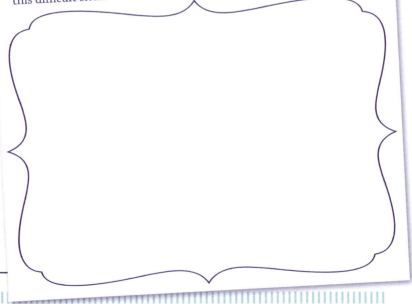

The Gratitude Connection

Developing confidence in your abilities starts with an optimistic point of view. But sometimes developing a positive outlook is difficult. Maybe you are dealing with some very difficult things in your life. There may be health or economic issues that you have to deal with every day. Or maybe there are issues of abuse and neglect. Sometimes your problems feel serious even though they are really just the smaller day-to-day difficulties of growing up, like girl drama and dating problems.

Whatever obstacles you face, these hard times can eat away at your confidence little by little until you find yourself struggling to believe anything positive about yourself. When this happens, staying the course on the journey inward is the last thing you'll be thinking about. These are the times when giving up sure seems a lot easier, when conforming to the masses and losing yourself may seem like attractive choices.

But giving in to what's hard and letting go of your dreams completely is never a good idea in the long run.

Fortunately, there are a few small things you can do that will boost your confidence and help you refocus your attention to the positive aspects of your life.

Maya Angelou, one of the most inspirational writers of the 20th century, speaks often of gratitude. In her writings, she links gratitude and a positive attitude to building an internal confidence and developing the strength to push through the hard times. And I couldn't agree more. Optimism and confidence go hand in hand, and both are enhanced through the development of a grateful heart.

Being grateful is a tricky thing at times, especially when it feels like the world is conspiring against you. This is when a gratitude journal can make all the difference.

Have you ever noticed that once you start focusing on bad things, all you see are bad things? And when you focus on the positive, you feel better and your confidence soars? The same is true with gratitude. If you focus on what is lacking in your life, all you see, all you feel, is that *lack*. But, if you make a shift and begin to focus on what you have, you open your heart and mind to embracing a more confident point of view.

Developing mindful gratitude, as I call it, requires a daily commitment to seeking and acknowledging what you are grateful for. This can include little things like being grateful for your kitten's soft fur that feels so nice when you stroke her back, as well as bigger things like being thankful for your mom who worked all day, came home and made a healthy dinner, and still managed to find time to curl your hair for the Homecoming dance. What you are grateful for is not important. Finding things to be grateful for every day—that's the focus.

Take a moment and start your own gratitude journal. Make a goal to find five things every day that you are sincerely thankful for. As you begin to deliberately seek out the positive, your mind will reward you with increased confidence and a more positive outlook.

Developing a positive perspective will be discussed again later in the book. For now, thinking about the things you're grateful for is the ideal first step toward developing the confidence necessary to pursue your dreams, even when it is hard (and trust me, there are times when it will be very hard!).

The Girl Guide Activity #11

My Gratitude Journal

Directions: Follow the steps below to create your own gratitude journal.

1. Make a special section in your journal for your gratitude journal.

2. Every night before bed, write 5-10 things you are thankful for. These don't have to be big things. They can be as simple as being thankful that it didn't rain. Anything, really.

3. Do this every night until you've developed the habit of looking for things that bring out your grateful heart.

Confidence and Pride

Have you ever met those people who are always confident about every single thing in life? They never seem to doubt themselves or get worried, even when it seems like they should be. Being confident in your abilities is important. But being realistic is also important. The trick is learning to take a positive outlook that's rooted in what's true and real for you.

As you start learning to discern between authentic confidence and false pride, it's important to understand the difference between the two. Confidence is defined as having the belief that you can accomplish what you set out to do. It means that you have a fervent belief in your ability to prosper in certain roles and perform at a high level.

Pride is a similar construct and, in this case, means having respect for your own accomplishments or a high level of esteem regarding your performance. Pride and confidence are two sides of a coin, really. Confidence is the feeling before the task, whereas pride is the feeling after. Pride can increase confidence for future tasks, which can result in stronger pride. And so on and so on.

But both confidence and pride can be misguided, driven by the illusion of competence and success. Such overconfidence and false pride can have disastrous results. Take, for example, the girl who has extreme confidence in her abilities to sing. In her mind, she is certain to be the next American Idol. Every time she sings in front of the mirror, her vision of herself grows, as does her pride, until she is certain she is the best thing to ever happen to music.

Until she tries out for a singing competition.

Having had no training and no performance experience, her opinions may not be the most accurate in terms of her talent compared to global talent within the field of song. But she doesn't have this perspective. She can't. Her opinion is skewed, based on her limited experiences. She goes to the audition and is mortified when she not only doesn't make it into the competition, but her peers are less than complimentary about her abilities. Thrown into internal chaos, she decides to quit singing all together, despite how happy it made her feel.

This is a horrible situation. But one that can be avoided with a little guidance.

The truth of her situation is that her confidence and pride, although good and a source of strength, were somewhat misguided. They were not rooted in the truth of her situation. And when she experienced a lack of success, the false pride and confidence ultimately failed.

So what could she have done?

First, she could broaden her experiences so as to better judge her strengthens and weaknesses. Second, she should stop dealing in absolutes. Much of the time, false pride is developed as a by-product of black-and-white thinking, or absolutes. The girl in the story thought she was "the best" at singing, failing to recognize that such statements are inherently false. There are always people who are better than we imagine. No one is ever the best, really.

So instead of dealing in absolutes, it's important to develop a true sense of confidence and pride, firmly rooted in an accurate reflection of your own strengths and accomplishments.

> *I hate it when people say "great job" when I haven't done anything. It feels fake. But, tell me why I've done a good job on something and yes . . . I love hearing that!* —MacKenzie, age 14

In the previous section, you developed a gratitude journal that will help you remember to focus on the positive. Now, you will use that positive outlook to begin to acknowledge your strengths and accomplishments. Start a new journal section in which to track your accomplishments, no matter how small. Try to find three things every day that you accomplished that you can be proud of. As with the gratitude journal, these can be small accomplishments, like making your bed without being told, or bigger ones, like striking out a batter during softball practice. The important thing is to begin to cultivate the habit of acknowledging your successes.

The Girl Guide Activity #12

My Accomplishments Journal

Directions: Use the steps that follow to recognize all of your accomplishments in life.

1. Similar to the gratitude journal, set up a special section in your journal in which you highlight your accomplishments.

2. Every day, find at least one thing you accomplished. It could be something small, like doing your chores without being told, or bigger, like making the swim team.

3. Decorate the pages with positive words, and be your own best cheerleader.

Now that you have begun to both cultivate a positive attitude and acknowledge your true successes, it's time to use your accomplishments to propel you toward your dreams. The first step is seeing the connection between your accomplishments and the skills needed to excel in those areas. Later, I will show you how to use those skills in areas you struggle with. But first, create a bank of your skills. This bank will help you overcome some of the hurdles you may face on the journey inward.

Worksheet #10: Skills Bank

Directions: Using the accomplishment journal you've created, write down different accomplishments and what part of your life they relate to (domain). Then figure out what skills you needed and used in order to achieve your accomplishments.

Accomplishment	Domain	Skills needed
Got a good grade on my math test	School	– Organizational skills – Math skills – Memory skills – Dedication and commitment

Note to Self: Just Be You

Stay strong! Don't let all those people who don't understand you make you change who you are. It'll take a long time to recover if you lose yourself now. Don't compare yourself to others. Listen to the people who build you up, not those who tear you apart. Keep an honest perspective on yourself and keep growing. Keep learning. Keep expanding who you are and what you are capable of doing. You can do anything you put your mind to, but remember to give yourself a break when things don't go exactly as planned. Find your dream and live it! —Rev. Mona Chicks

Throughout this chapter, you learned about maintaining a positive attitude and developing confidence. You also learned the difference between real confidence and false pride. As we move into the next chapter and look at overcoming life's difficulties, I want you to reflect on your own confidence and the things that lead to false pride, as well as low confidence, for you.

My Voice

Keeping in mind the authentic you inside, answer the following:

▶ What are some areas where you tend to have little confidence? What can you do to raise your confidence in these areas?

▶ What are some areas where you tend to be overconfident? (Maybe these are areas where you typically excel.) Is it wrong to be overly confident? Why or why not?

▶ What is the connection between a positive attitude and confidence in yourself?

Chapter 8

The Art of Plan B

> *My mother always told me to plan ahead for emergencies. And while I never gave much thought about it, I did heed her advice and made back-up plans for things like college and even my social life. Good thing, since my life is very different than what I'd expected.* —Aggie, age 18

No matter how strong your confidence and pride in your abilities becomes, life will still throw its fair share of curveballs your way. That's where having a Plan B (or C, D, and E) comes in handy. When you get derailed on your journey toward your unique voice and your dreams, which may happen periodically, you have a couple of choices—give up or forge a new path. Being prepared and remaining flexible in your thinking helps give you a chance to develop a new plan when the situation calls for it.

This chapter will focus on remaining flexible, adapting to new situations, and learning to take constructive criticism without letting it demoralize you.

Let's start with another scenario to get the ball rolling.

What Would You Do?

You've always had one dream in life—to dance! You want to join the New York City Ballet and perform. You started talking ballet classes at the age of 2, practicing hours every day. Now that you are in high school, you've convinced your parents to let you pursue your dream, starting with an audition with the Joffrey Ballet School. You've practiced and worked very hard preparing for the big day. You just know you'll get in and the journey toward your dream of dancing in New York will come true.

Until . . .

The day before you are to leave for the audition, you tear your MCL while practicing. The pain is excruciating. Worse, the doctors and your parents have all told you that you can't audition. You are devastated. Every hope, every dream was riding on this audition. And now, you have no idea when you will be able to move to New York to dance.

What do you do? Let your knee heal and try to audition later in the season? Try a different school? Come up with another plan for dancing? Cry for days?

Take a moment and write down what you would do if this happened to you.

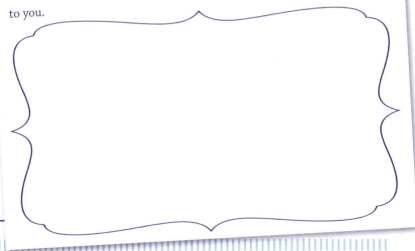

What Is a Plan B?

As the scenario pointed out, life doesn't always cooperate with our plans. Things can happen to prevent us from moving in a direction we choose—sometimes due to things we can control, and often due to things we cannot control. Regardless of how we get off track, having an alternative plan (or two) enables a few things to happen.

First, the development of an alternative plan will help ease your stress as you take the journey toward your dreams. No longer in an all-or-nothing situation, having alternative plans enables you to enjoy the journey a bit more and go with the flow of life, without trying to bend life to your will.

Alternative plans also teach the valuable skill of adaptability—by going through the process of making a secondary or tertiary plan, you acknowledge the reality that things may not always happen the way you anticipate, but that doesn't mean you can't achieve what you've set out to do. You simply need to be *willing* to try another route, a new map.

Work through Worksheet #11 and begin to come up with alternative paths to achieve your goals.

As you begin to practice finding all of the different ways to get from point A to point B, I want you to complete Activity #13, A Storybook Ending.

Worksheet #11: Planning for Plan B

Directions: List your goals from Worksheet #2 and two possible ways to achieve each one.

Goal	Plan A	Plan B
School Goal #1 Pass my math final	– Study for 15 minutes a night – Redo any problems on the quiz I got wrong – Ask my teacher for help if I get confused	– Form a study group – Attend the extra study sessions at school
School Goal #1		
School Goal #2		
Personal Goal #1		
Personal Goal #2		
Long-Term Goal #1		
Long-Term Goal #2		

A Storybook Ending

Directions: Pick one (or all) of the following activities to help you see how not everything has a perfect, storybook ending.

1. Using one of your favorite fairy tales, rewrite it from an object's point of view. For example, rewrite the story of Goldilocks and the Three Bears from the point of view of the little bear's chair. How did the story change? How did your understanding of the story change?

2. Rewrite the ending of a well-known story or your favorite book, creating a newscast to tell what happens differently to the characters (try videotaping this or making a podcast). Did this activity change your perspective of the story and its characters?

3. Try to find three or four stories, movies, or TV shows that are retellings of popular stories from alternative perspectives. What did those shows teach you about the story? Consider blogging about how retellings of popular stories in media today helps you change your perspective of your goals and dreams.

Overcoming Obstacles

In addition to teaching you flexibility, learning to think about alternative options toward a common goal can also help provide a foundation for overcoming whatever obstacles may come your way.

Handling adversity is more than just pushing through the hard stuff. It is also about staying open and flexible to opportunities that present themselves to you. Helen Keller was a great example of this. She often spoke of remaining open to all of life's journeys. As a woman who overcame some pretty intense obstacles, I think she was on to something.

Life does present its challenges. But every time we are successful in something, even the tiniest of things, we are afforded an opportunity to take what we've learned and build on it. That is why it is so important to celebrate your little victories, so that you can begin to see the skills you are acquiring and apply them to new situations.

Using the accomplishment journal and skill bank you developed in Chapter 7, take a moment to use some of your previous accomplishments and the skills you learned from them to create a road map toward your dreams in Activity #14.

Another part of overcoming obstacles involves being able to listen to your parents and friends when they offer advice and constructive criticism. Yes, I know, it is very hard to hear criticism, even when it is meant to help. Oftentimes, you may only hear the negative aspects of what is being said, instead of hearing all of the positives and the advice being offered. You may get "stuck" in your opinion, unable to see all of the alternative paths you can take toward your destination. Or you may just be feeling attacked and want to respond in kind.

A Map for Life

Directions: Use the ideas that follow to help you make a road map for your life.

1. Using your journal, list some of the goals, accomplishments, and skills you have acquired based on what you've written for the previous worksheets.

2. Using that information, draw a road map that takes you from where you are toward your dreams identified in your dream poster.

3. Label the parts of the journey with the skills you will need to get there.

4. Color in the page and decorate it with things that remind you both of your journey and your skills.

5. Redraw your map anytime you feel like you are losing your way.

Regardless of why taking constructive criticism is difficult for you, being willing to listen to advice and opposing points of view is an important aspect of becoming flexible and adapting to different situations.

Tool #5

Staying Open to Ideas

- Remain quiet and focus on the person speaking.
- Try to listen with your eyes and your ears.
- Don't react to things that you may not like.
- Try to find one new idea you can try.
- Don't personalize the advice. Constructive criticism is about helping, not hurting.

Note to Self: Reach for the Stars

Follow your dreams. Ignore the voices of those who would tell you to play it safe, to take the easy route, to not aim for the stars in case you fall. Instead, dust yourself off and try again. Embrace your heritage—the strong, capable, independent, and fierce women who also aimed for the stars and who, when they fell, got up, dusted themselves off, and tried again. —Rebekah Graham

Being adaptable and willing to alter your plans when needed are skills that can keep you on the journey toward your dreams. Like the old adage says, life really is a journey—one filled with good and bad, ups and downs, happiness and sorrow. This is a given. How you deal with the adversity and the skills you develop in the process—those are the things that will shape your outcome.

The next section refocuses our attention back toward perspective and optimism, building on some of the previously learned skills. But first, take a moment to reflect on your own adaptability skills.

My Voice

Keeping in mind the authentic you inside, answer the following:

- ▶ Do you believe in developing back-up plans for life? Why or why not?
- ▶ How do you feel when someone tries to give you constructive criticism? Is it hard for you to listen to the feedback? Does your mind wander as you try to think of all of the ways the feedback doesn't apply to you? How can you prevent that from happening?
- ▶ Do you think it is important to be flexible in life? Why or why not?

Chapter 9

Half-Full or Half-Empty: The Power of Perspective

> *I must admit, I put myself down a lot. I know I shouldn't—at least that is what everyone tells me. But I can't help it. I just struggle to quiet the noise in my head.* —Nadia, age 17

"Perspicere" is the Latin verb meaning "to see clearly," and is the root of perspective. Having a healthy perspective means you are accurately assessing the situation at hand. Believe me, this is much harder to accomplish than it may sound. More often, your perspective on a situation is skewed by everything including your current emotional status, assumptions about the event that you may or may not be aware of, and the self-talk existing in your head. All of these things taint your perspective and can, at times, prevent you from seeing a situation clearly.

This next scenario involves perspective and what happens when you misinterpret a situation.

What Would You Do?

You and Jody have been best friends since second grade. But recently, you haven't felt as close. Sure, you both go to the same school, have the same teachers, and hang out together at lunch. But something has changed.

You try to talk with Jody but all she does is get mad and walk away. Eventually, after 2 weeks of asking her to tell you what is bothering her, she stops sitting with you at lunch altogether.

She joins the "popular" table, avoids you in the hall, and asks to have her seat moved in class. And that's just the beginning.

Over the next few weeks you catch her whispering to her new friends and think you hear your name amongst the chatter. You stare at her, but she avoids looking at you completely. Pretty soon, you don't see her at all.

A few days later, a rumor starts spreading about you. You are convinced Jody had something to do with it.

What do you do? Confront her? Start a rumor about her? Ignore everything?

Take a moment and write down how you would handle this situation.

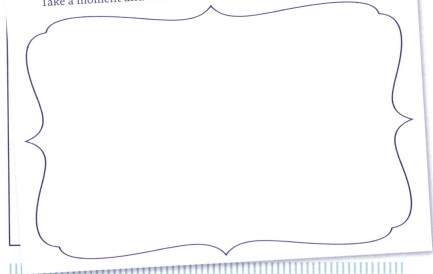

Perception and Context

I started this chapter by talking about the art of seeing clearly, or perspective. Your specific perception of a situation influences the way you handle that situation. Perception is based on things you see, hear, and feel, as well as the way you think about those things. In other words, whether or not your day is a *good day* has more to do with your perception of it than anything else.

How you perceive events is influenced by the context of the situation. For example, if I am in a farmer's market and I take an apple that I did not pay for, then I am a thief. If, however, I take that apple because I have not eaten in several days, although I am still a thief, the situation is more complicated than initially presented. Such is true with most events in life.

Do you remember when I said that it is important to be flexible, to recognize that life is seldom black and white, but more often many shades of grey? This is because of perception and context.

For example, it is common in the United States to point with our index finger when we are indicating a specific thing, like where something is located. However, to many other cultures in the world, pointing with your index finger is a serious affront, often interpreted as a sign of disrespect. In one context, the action was appropriate, in another it was not. Context is what separates the two events, context and perspective.

Take a moment to work through the What Is Happening? worksheet and come up with as many different reasons why the different events listed may have occurred. The more you can come up with, the better.

The Girl Guide

Worksheet #12: What Is Happening?

Directions: Take a moment and read each statement, then think about the particular event. Can you figure out what happened just before? How about immediately after? Write down what happened before and after each event listed and try to determine all of the potential meanings for the events. I've completed the first example for you.

Event	What happened before the event (context)	What happened after	Possible meanings for the event
Your BFF yells at you at lunch.	She spoke to her boyfriend.	She ran off to the bathroom.	– She got into an argument with her boyfriend and vented at me. – She found out something bad about her boyfriend or his family. – She got a text about something else that upset her. – She ran to the bathroom for "female" issues.
The teacher tells you to stay after class.			
Your mom accuses you of giving her attitude.			
Your sister comes into your room and takes your magazine.			
Your friend stops answering your texts and phone calls.			
A boy you like looks at you and then whispers quietly to his friends.			
You walk into a store with your friends right as two people you know from school start laughing.			
You stop running in PE and get yelled at by the teacher.			

»

What have you learned from looking at events in this way? Take a moment to write down your thoughts.

White Noise

Perception is influenced by more than context and the information from our five senses. As I mentioned earlier, it is also influenced by the self-talk we engage in internally—the constant noise in our head that tells us about the world.

Most of you have a lot of chatter going on in your thoughts all of the time—a running commentary about everything and everyone. This is not unusual. But, it can be distracting. And depending on what that voice in your head is saying, it can be damaging too.

Earlier, I spent a lot of time asking you to learn to listen to the voice in your head—the one that knows your heart's desire and your dreams; the one that can lead you along your journey to your authentic self. The voice that engages in the endless chatter in your thoughts is *not* the same voice. Learning to tell the difference between the two is difficult, but it can be done.

To start, you must learn to tease out what is true about your running commentary and what is not. My guess is that most of what you find in your thoughts will not be true—merely an incessant dialogue highlighting your doubts and perceived failures, spinning in an endless loop that eventually sounds like nothing but white noise. The more you put yourself down, the more you listen to others and let them tear you down, the louder that voice inside can become.

Fortunately, you can learn to quiet the noise and discover when it's valid or not. My mother used to tell me "Act on what you know, not on what you think or assume." In other words, take the time to look at what you are reacting to and make sure that what you *think* happened has actually happened.

Here's an example: You are upset over your best friend from another school's recent change in behavior. She used to text you nightly, chatting about life. Then she stopped. Just stopped. No rhyme or reason why. Nothing. Just the end to a friendship. At least, that's how it seemed. In truth, she was grounded for 3 weeks. Because you only communicated via text and phone before now, you had no way of knowing what actually happened. You assumed that something was wrong with your friendship, when in truth, everything was fine. When you act on what you know, not what you assume, you start to discern all of the reasons why things happen and begin to seek truth and stay away from assumptions.

This next tool is one way to begin to differentiate what is true versus what is false in your mind.

Tool #6

Is It True?

- ▸ Take a moment to listen to the self-talk going on in your head. What message is your brain telling you?
- ▸ How do you know the message is correct?
- ▸ Look outward for proof of the accuracy of the message. If you can't find any, then it is time to change the inner message.
- ▸ Tell yourself the true message. Write it in your journal and repeat it several times.

Sometimes it's hard to shift the noise running through our thoughts from an endless stream of negativity toward something more positive. Activity #15 is all about finding the silver lining and turning negatives into positives. For example, maybe you are telling yourself that you are too talkative in class. Rather than focusing on that, compliment yourself for being uber-curious, and figure out a way to not be disruptive in class. Or you are always the last picked in PE and internally you decide it is because you're clumsy. Instead, think about something positive about your physical skills. Maybe you are good in the water, but not running the track. Or maybe you are good at wrestling, but not at baseball. Whatever it is, try to replace the negative chatter with something more positive. Assuming a positive mental perspective will help you stay on the path toward your authentic self and navigate the rough patches with ease.

> *Okay, I'll admit it—I struggle with confidence. And staying positive. But learning to be aware of what I tell myself has really helped me get a handle on everything. Try it.* —Shamonique, age 18

Take a moment to make yourself a set of cards like those in Activity #15. Pull these out and read them anytime you hear yourself engaging in negative self-talk. In no time, you will shift from a negative to positive point of view.

As I mentioned previously, a positive perspective, both internal and external, is vital on the journey to the self. Not only does it help you stay strong and overcome life's curveballs, but it also helps you see the world from many different angles. This in turn allows you to hone your empathy skills, increase your problem-solving abilities, and build relationships. By seeing the world from different perspectives, you are able to seek creative solutions to problems, as well as understand why things happen as they do.

I <3 Me

Directions: Use the directions that follow to help you discover what you love about yourself.

1. Turn to a new page in your journal. Make a list of the ways in which you are a good friend and a great person. Refer to your accomplishment journal and your skill bank if needed.

2. Make another list of your interests, anything that is uniquely you.

3. Using the information from the lists, take several index or note cards and write positive statements about you and your interests/accomplishments all on one side of the cards.

4. Turn the cards over and decorate them in inspiring ways, something that makes you smile and speaks to the inner you inside.

5. Make at least 5 cards, each one focused on a different aspect of you.

6. Make new cards anytime you accomplish something new or develop a new interest.

7. Refer to the cards anytime you are feeling down about yourself.

Take a moment and review the Fresh Perspectives activity from Chapter 6. Repeat the activity with different pictures any time you need to remind yourself to see something from a fresh point of view.

Note to Self: Perspective Is Everything

There is no meaning to anything other than the meaning you ascribe to it. So if you are feeling out of sorts with the world, your friends, your family—take a look at your point of view on things and see if it needs adjusting. After all, you are the only one who can change your perspective. —Judi Warren

You've spent the last several chapters learning to cultivate a positive attitude, appreciate your various accomplishments, see the world from many perspectives, and develop many alternative solutions or paths on the journey to yourself. All of these skills have one thing in common—together they enable you to take control over your life and mold it into what you want it to be.

In the next section, you will learn about your emotions and the impact of your emotional reactions on the journey you are undertaking toward your authentic self.

Before we jump into that, however, take a moment to reflect on the things you have learned in this chapter about perspective.

My Voice

Keeping in mind the authentic you inside, reflect on and answer the following:

- When I am alone, or my mind is drifting off at school, do I notice that I talk to myself a lot? What do I say?
- Do I get stuck or rigid in my thinking when I make plans, then struggle to adjust my plans? Why or why not?
- Is staying positive important to me? Why or why not?
- Do I believe that I have what it takes to get through life's difficulties? Why or why not?
- When I think about myself, what are the first two words that come to mind? Why did I pick those particular words?

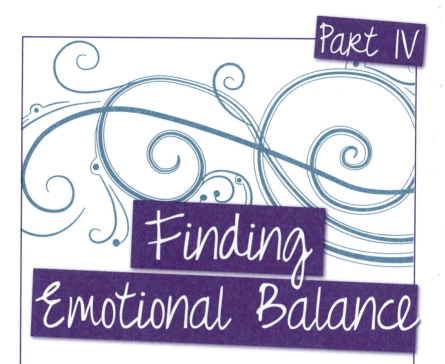

Part IV

Finding Emotional Balance

Sometimes life can become overwhelming, especially as you make the transition from childhood into adulthood. Being highly emotional during this time is not unusual. However, how you deal with your emotions can influence your ability to find your voice and achieve your goals. It can affect your overall resiliency.

The next chapters take a look at all of the aspects of your emotional self, from how you initially react to adversity, to how long it takes you to bounce back, to what strategies you can use to make the process easier on you and everyone else.

To start things off, it's important to know how you typically react to the things life may throw your way, so take Quiz #4!

My Feelings

1. When I get mad, I stay mad for a long time.

    ☐ True   ☐ False

2. I can't think clearly when I am upset about things.

    ☐ True   ☐ False

3. When I'm emotional, I don't make clear decisions.

    ☐ True   ☐ False

4. I get more upset over problems at school than problems with my friends.

    ☐ True   ☐ False

5. When I am very emotional, my feelings are overwhelming.

    ☐ True   ☐ False

Chapter 10

Understanding Emotional Sensitivity

> I get really stressed out at times—everyone does. The key is remembering to relax. The sooner I can relax, the better. For everyone. —Alana, age 16

The last few sections have been dedicated to understanding and developing your social relationships and goals in life. This next section is all about emotions. As stated in the introduction, being highly emotional during this time in your life is normal. How you react to the emotional upheaval is what's important.

We'll begin this leg of the journey with understanding when and how you react to periods of stress. You will explore the things that trigger your emotions and the ways in which you respond. To start, take a look at the following scenario.

What Would You Do?

You have a major language arts project due in a few weeks. Being organized, you get it done with a week to spare. Except for one problem . . . you hate it. Like, completely hate it. So even though it's due in a matter of days, and even though your schedule is slammed with other activities, you decide to completely redo the project.

You work tirelessly on everything you have going on. One night, the day before the project is due, your mom comes into your room and asks you about your day. You respond by screaming at her and telling her to stop pressuring you. She leaves, and you feel guilty. You know she didn't do anything wrong. You were just feeling overwhelmed.

What do you do? Go and apologize? Pretend nothing happened and let your mom get over any hurt feelings she has? Desperately try to finish the project?

Take a moment and write down what you would do to navigate through scholastic stress.

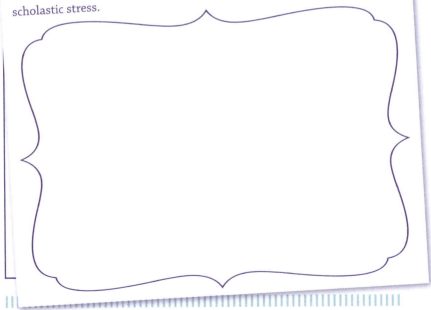

Understanding Emotions

It is no surprise that you are emotional. Very emotional. It goes along with being a teen. Dealing with your emotions and learning how to discuss, manage, and use them can make the difference between being a slave to the emotional rollercoaster that often defines adolescence and being the master of your feelings.

In order to manage your emotions, you must learn how to recognize and talk about them. The best way to do this is with some form of an emotional vocabulary, or having the right words to appropriately describe your feelings that enable you to communicate when you are overwhelmed and frustrated without blowing up at people.

Developing an emotional vocabulary is a way of putting something intangible, like your feelings, into definable terms and creating a little distance from it. This enables you to look at your emotional status without becoming absorbed by your feelings. Furthermore, picking a word or phrase that you can use with friends and family to alert them to when you are becoming overwhelmed can enable you to manage your emotions before they get the better of you. In my house, we use the word "spinning" to represent when things have become too overwhelming, when we are feeling out of control and overly volatile, or when we can't manage our emotional reactions. My daughters and I use the word to easily alert each other that we are an emotional mess at the moment. The word, used in conjunction with taking a break and other relaxation techniques, helps the entire household work through those highly emotional times.

Developing and using an emotional vocabulary requires practice before it can become something you do naturally. Take a moment to complete Worksheet #13 and begin to develop your own emotional word bank. When you're done, pick a phrase that you can easily use to indicate that you are overwhelmed and share it with your friends and family. The next time you feel yourself escalating, try using the phrase. Although it will no doubt feel awkward at first, the more you use your emotional vocabulary and the more you begin to manage your emotions, the easier it gets.

How Do I React?

Developing your emotional vocabulary is a great first step, but it means nothing if you have no idea when you are stressed and frustrated. Oh sure, you probably know when you are beyond mad. But knowing when you are at the early stages of stress is something totally different.

Let's start by understanding what stress and frustration mean. Merriam-Webster defines stress as "a physical or emotional factor that causes tension on the mind or body." It is neither positive nor negative, simply any act that throws the body out of equilibrium.

People vary in their responses to stress based on age, developmental level, cultural norms, and tolerance for changes to their internal homeostatic state. Young children respond to stress with behaviors that mimic the onset of illness, like being clingy or experiencing changes in sleep and eating patterns. Children in elementary school may react by complaining of physical ailments or general moodiness. Teens do the same thing, only with more emotion.

If you'll notice, there are physical reactions associated with all of these descriptions of stress responses. That's because stress, or internal tension, almost always has a corresponding physical reaction that taps into your biology and results in a variety of physical

My Emotional Vocabulary

Directions: Look at each adjective. For each word, write your feelings and draw or find a picture to represent that feeling.

Mood	Description	Picture
Happy		
Sad		
Angry		
Scared		
Excited		
Anxious		
Frustrated		
Stressed		
Joyful		

Pick one or two words that best describe you when you are frustrated or stressed. Use these words to prompt others when you are beginning to lose control of your emotions.

changes including increased heart rate, sweating, digestive changes, and even changes to your brain's ability to think. These changes can significantly impact your functioning if you do not get a handle on the stress at the earliest stages.

But how can you recognize your early warning signals of anxiety, stress, and frustration? How can you warn others that you are becoming overwhelmed when you don't recognize it for yourself?

The trick is getting in touch with your own individual stress response and then fine-tuning your perception to recognize it. Complete Worksheet #14 to discover and chart your own stress response. Knowing how to react will enable you to prevent extreme emotional mood swings before they get the better of you.

As I said before, knowing your response cycle will help you better manage your emotions. But it won't happen overnight. It takes a lot of practice to become mindful of your feelings and responses. Practice the skill daily and see the difference it begins to make over time.

Understanding Triggers

In addition to understanding your emotional reactions and developing an emotional vocabulary, it is helpful to understand your triggers. We all have things that get under our skin, things that can make us angry or frustrated very quickly. It is important to understand your personal triggers so you can begin to plan ahead for the response.

So what kinds of things typically trigger you? Most girls are triggered by changes at home or school, friendship drama, relationship issues, unclear expectations, and fear of impending events like going to high school or learning to drive. Things like changes

How Do I React?

Directions: Take a moment and focus on how you react to various emotional situations like tests, arguments, or even dramatic movies. Then, answer the questions below and determine your typical method of reacting to things. Be sure to answer the questions at the end.

1. Watch a high-impact movie or play a video game and answer the following questions:

   a. How does your body feel during the action scenes? Where do you "feel" the action in your body? (Does your jaw tense? Do your palms sweat?)

   b. How does your mind feel during action scenes? Are you overly focused? Do you feel tired?

2. The next time you have a test, think about the following:

   a. Do you have any similar symptoms to how you felt in the movie in your body?

   b. What do you find yourself thinking before a test?

3. The next time you feel strong emotions—happy or sad—ask yourself the following:

   a. Do you feel similar to how you felt during the movie?

   b. What is your mind thinking?

Once you are finished, reflect on your answers. What kinds of things make you react the strongest? How do you physically react? What are you thinking? Take a moment to write down your thoughts about your reactions.

in appearance, new feelings of attraction, and sudden conflict with your mother can also bring about stress-based reactions. Take a moment and complete the My Triggers worksheet to discover what events make you stressed.

Not all stress-inducing experiences cause the same reaction. Some things may make a friend anxious, but not bother you at all. Some things you may get very frustrated with, while others may only annoy you. Go back through the triggers you identified on the previous worksheet and indicate how upset the event makes you. Review the chart often as your tolerance and stress triggers will change over time.

Note to Self: Take Time to Think

Stop. Think. Decide. My daughter is very impulsive in her actions. She is in the gifted program and very book-smart. But she acts before she thinks. We have come up with these three steps for her, which help her to slow down and think through something. —S. R. Johannes

Worksheet #15: My Triggers

Directions: Take a moment to think about the things that cause you to have a strong emotional reaction. Then, write down the event and emotion(s). Rate each event 1-5 based on how emotional you become.

Event	Emotion(s)	How upset am I? (1 - not upset; 5 - extremely upset)
My friend lied to me.	Sad, angry, distrusting	3

Everyone gets stressed from time to time. And most often that stress can result in a lot of emotional drama. By learning how to talk about your feelings and tell others you are overwhelmed and by knowing what triggers you, you can begin to manage the emotions more effectively and slow down the rollercoaster ride. These skills will help as you face life's adversities and cultivate your authentic place in the world.

The next chapter explores what happens when you can't stop the emotions from overwhelming you completely. But before we get to that, take a moment to reflect on your own emotional sensitivity more closely.

My Voice

Take a moment to listen for your authentic voice and answer the following:

- Do you think you get upset more or less often than your friends? Why?
- Recall the last time you got really upset. What happened, and what did you do?
- How often are you out-of-control stressed or upset? What do you do when that happens?
- Are you satisfied with your emotional sensitivity? Does any aspect of it bother you? Why or why not?

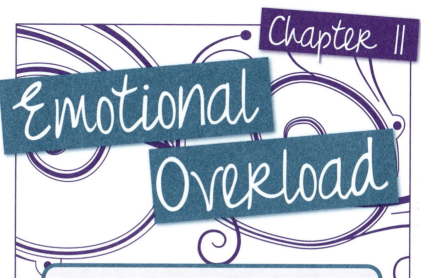

Chapter 11

Emotional Overload

All that emotional drama that happens in middle school—yeah, it's normal. But the sooner you learn to manage it, and your reactions, the easier life gets. Trust me. —Paige, age 17

Now that you know how and why you react to different things, it's time to take a look at what happens when you are completely overwhelmed. Some of you may feel guilty or engage in excessive negative self-talk. Some of you may obsess over the event, replaying your response over and over again. And some of you may become upset enough to engage in self-harm or hurt others.

Whatever is true for you, it is important to learn how you deal with the overload and what you can do to combat the negative impact of extreme emotional reactions.

This next scenario deals with one example of the more harmful effects of being emotionally overwhelmed. As you figure out what you would do in the situation, imagine your response to a similar set of events.

What Would You Do?

You and your friends are having lunch when something suddenly catches your attention. An old acquaintance is freaking out. She's screaming at a group of friends and throwing her backpack on the ground. She runs off, leaving a crowd of people in shock. As she passes you, you notice that her eyes are filled with tears, and she is hyperventilating. You know you should probably follow her; after all, she was a friend once.

What do you do? Follow her? Get help? Stay out of it since you haven't spoken in months?

Take a moment and jot down how you would handle this emotionally charged situation.

Becoming Overwhelmed

It happens to all of us sooner or later—you get so overwhelmed by your emotions that you lose it. Maybe you scream and yell, maybe you throw things. Maybe you even hurt someone, even yourself.

At these moments, all of the techniques you've worked on and all of your strategies for managing your emotions fail. Your words fail. Your ability to circumvent the tide of emotions is compromised. And you simply explode.

Your brain is a funny thing. When you are angry (or sad or frustrated), the part of your brain that makes rational decisions slows or stops. You literally can't think about calming down. Nor can you prevent the explosion from happening at this point. It's too late. Your only choice is to ride out the reaction and try to pull yourself together as quickly as you can.

The key is trying to catch the explosion before it happens. Use the strategies from the previous chapter to recognize your warning signs and diffuse the situation while you still can.

There are lots of tricks people use to calm themselves. Taking deep breaths, picturing something relaxing, taking a break—all of these things can help diffuse your frustration, anger, or pain and allow your brain time to think. And that can prevent the explosion from happening in the first place.

> *Man, do I have an anger problem when I'm stressed. I just can't help it . . . the more stressed I get, the more likely I am to yell for some reason.* —Shayna, age 16

Take a moment to read over the next tool, Stress Busters, and then complete the Reducing My Overload worksheet to develop your own plan for combating stress and managing your emotions when you are overwhelmed.

Stress Busters

- ▶ Practice healthy living. Get plenty of sleep, eat well, and exercise.
- ▶ Make your room a calming place.
- ▶ Practice one of these ways to relax:
  - ◇ *Deep breathing:* Take several slow, deep breaths in through your nose and out through your mouth.
  - ◇ *Breathing colors:* Take several deep breaths. On the inhalation, picture your favorite color. I use blue or pink. On the exhalation, imagine a dirty color. This is the color of the stress in your body. Continue slow steady breathing until the color you inhale matches the color you exhale.

- ▶ Learn strong communication skills and conflict resolution skills.
- ▶ Practice good boundaries (see Activity #4).

Learning From the Explosion

You've learned how to manage your emotions and diffuse the frustration before you get too overwhelmed—at least, most of the time. The rest of the time, despite your best efforts, you still let

Reducing My Overload

Directions: Take a few minutes to answer the questions below and evaluate the effectiveness of the stress busters you've been using. Be sure to answer the questions at the end.

1. How does your body feel? Do you have any tension anywhere?

2. How does your mind feel? Are you focused? Tired?

3. How are your emotions? Do you feel calm?

4. Have you tried any strategies to relax? Did they work?

5. What do you notice about how you feel right now?

6. What technique did you use? Was it effective?

Worksheet #16 Continued

Once you are finished, reflect on your answers. Were the stress busters you utilized effective? Why or why not? Take a moment to write down your thoughts on the particular stress busters you utilized and whether or not you plan to use them again.

your emotions get the better of you. It's important not to further complicate the situation by engaging in defeatist chatter or obsessing over your perceived mistakes over and over. Managing your emotions is not a foolproof endeavor. What's important is using these moments as opportunities to learn and improve your skills.

The best way to handle the post-explosion time is to reflect on what happened in a constructive way. That means not engaging in negative chatter, but using the reflection as a chance to learn a new way of responding or practicing the skill that you weren't able to use previously.

Debriefing, or analyzing what lead up to the explosion and how you responded, is similar to all of the self-reflection exercises you've been doing throughout this book. In Activity #16, you will look at the event, figure out what happened, and decide how you can change things to result in a different outcome. Debriefing after every explosion will help you reinforce the reaction skills you are trying to develop. This technique will also help you learn how to bounce back from setbacks more confidently and change your perspective to see them for what they really are—opportunities to learn.

Take a moment to create your own debriefing worksheet. Use it anytime you need to reflect on your behavior and change your response.

My Thinking Sheet

Directions: Work through the steps that follow to help you develop a way to track your reactions to emotional situations.

1. Using a plain piece of paper, list the following questions, leaving a space to answer them after you have an emotional explosion:

   a. What do I think happened?

   b. What was I feeling at the time?

   c. Did I feel like I was losing control? When?

   d. Did I try any strategies to calm down? What were they? What was the result?

   e. Things I noticed about my behavior:

   f. Things I noticed about my feelings:

   g. What I want to try next time:

2. Make a few copies of the questions and use them anytime you need to reflect on your behavior. Or, add them to the Notes section of your phone so you have them easily available whenever an explosion occurs.

3. Once you have completed each sheet, paste it into your journal or e-mail yourself the answers. After you have several completed sets of questions, look at them to see if you can discover any patterns to your behavior.

Note to Self: Try New Things

Never be afraid to try something new.

One of the tricky things about being told you're good at something is the way it can take over who you are and how you spend your time. Perhaps you're a talented writer or a star soccer player. Perhaps you've been playing the violin since you were a toddler. Your peers admire you. Adults compliment you. It feels good. Comfortable.

I'm not suggesting that you abandon any of that. But I would encourage you to keep your mind open to other things you may want to try—even things at which you think you might not be as good.

Why? First, you may just surprise yourself and discover a new talent. Second, you may learn something that makes you better at the things you already do well. For me, the more important reason to try new things is that it gives you a special kind of courage that broadens your view of the world and the contribution you can make to it.

—Stasia Ward Kehoe

In this chapter, you explored what it means to be completely overwhelmed and how you would respond. You also looked at a scenario asking what you would do when faced with someone who is emotionally unstable. Take a moment to reflect on your emotional status and the kinds of things that can push you over the edge. We'll talk about achieving and maintaining emotional equilibrium in the next chapter.

My Voice

Keeping in mind your authentic perspective, answer the following:

- ▸ Think about a time when you made a mistake. What did you do?
- ▸ Think about a time when you were in trouble—big trouble. What happened and what did you do?
- ▸ What types of situations make you confused? Where do you go for help?
- ▸ Think about a time when you were emotionally overloaded. How did you act? How did you recover?
- ▸ Think about your most extreme emotions. What do they look like? How do you manage them? Do they scare you?

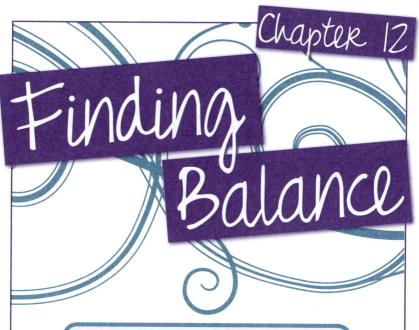

Chapter 12

Finding Balance

It's hard to remember that anxiety isn't uncommon and doesn't define you. —Maggie, age 13

Balance . . . such an easy concept and, yet, so hard to achieve most of the time. In the last two chapters you discovered what being emotionally sensitive means, how easy it is to become overwhelmed, and a few tools to combat the more difficult aspects of being emotional. Now it's time to develop the skills to stay in balance with your emotions—to use them to help you on your journey toward authenticity and adulthood, but not allow them to completely overwhelm your ability to cope, as can sometimes happen.

Before we begin to explore the difficult elements of achieving balance, take a moment and reflect on the following scenario.

What Would You Do?

You are typically a calm person, the one everyone turns to in an emergency. Nothing ever gets under your skin or rattles you. At least, that *used* to be true. Recently, something has changed—your heart now races before a test, you worry about things that you never thought of before, like what people are saying about you or how they are looking at you, and you carry a general feeling of unease most days.

You really want to get back to that calm state you used to feel, but you can't seem to find that place or be that girl.

What do you do? Talk to your mom or school counselor? Tell your friends? Suffer in silence hoping it's just some weird phase? Nothing?

Take a moment and write down what you would do if you found yourself suddenly unable to cope with life's stressors.

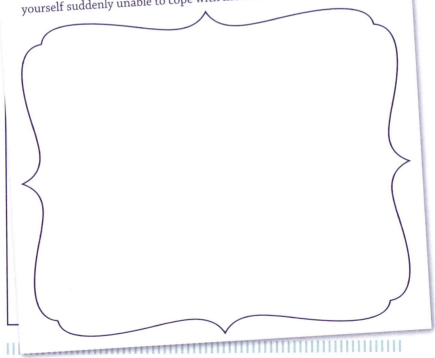

Developing Coping Skills

You've learned about stress and frustration, how you respond to stress, and what triggers you. You've also learned how to deal with overload and some typical tools for reducing your stress. Now, let's further explore coping skills and why they are so important.

Most negative behavior comes as a result of a person's reaction to what is happening around her. If her typical way of coping with things becomes compromised or overwhelmed, she will more likely engage in some form of negative behavior, some way to either get a need met or get out of the situation.

For example, if you are new to a school and haven't yet made any friends, you may feel a lot of apprehension about finding a place to eat lunch. You may get overwhelmed by the noise in the cafeteria, by the feeling that everyone is looking at you, and by the fear of not having a group of friends to connect with. Your senses may go on high-alert, making everything seem louder and more intense. You may begin to sweat or feel your back and jaw tighten. Eventually, if you haven't been able to calm this physical response, you may experience the overwhelming need to leave the cafeteria in search of someplace calm. You may do this simply by walking out. But if you are overwhelmed, you could push someone or otherwise cause a disturbance in order to exit the area. It all depends on how overwhelmed you are and your existing coping strategies.

In the previous chapters, you explored your own stress response and typical reactions. Now I want you to develop your own unique coping strategies. Look back at Worksheet #15. Think about the way you would respond to the various scenarios listed. Be sure to think about your extreme responses. Then develop a list of three things you can do in each of the scenarios in the next worksheet, My Coping Plan.

Worksheet #17: My Coping Plan

Directions: Pulling from Worksheet #15, My Triggers, complete this worksheet to develop an action plan for each triggering event.

Trigger	My Response	Action Plan
My friend yelled at me.	I felt angry and yelled back.	– Take a deep breath. – If needed, close my eyes until I am calm. – Ask her what is wrong in a calm voice.

Healthy Living Revisited

Having a reaction plan is a great way to deal with most of life's stressors. But in order for the plan to have the best success, it's important to fine-tune some of the skills you learned earlier in the book, including developing healthy lifestyle habits and boundaries.

In Chapter 3, you spent a lot of time developing the healthy habits needed to cope with life and help you on your inner journey. I want you to go back and read the tools and activities you completed in that chapter. If you haven't completed any of them, take a moment to do that as well.

Once you have reviewed the principles of healthy living, take a moment to develop a personal tool sheet like in Activity #17 you can use to remind yourself of the things you need to stay in balance and to create a healthy lifestyle that can become part of your normal routine.

Mindfulness

Another component of being in balance involves mindfulness. This refers to the ability to pay attention to the present moment without judgment. In other words, knowing what you are doing without placing judgment on your actions.

Mindfulness enables you to become aware of any negative chatter you are telling yourself, as well as any behaviors or habits that are counterproductive or pulling you away from your dreams and goals.

Becoming mindful takes a lot of practice. It is easy to misinterpret our behaviors and actions, making negative judgments about ourselves without realizing we have even done that.

Activity #17

My Life Tools

1. Using your journal or something similar, list some of the things you can do to reduce your emotional responses to things.

2. Find or draw pictures that reflect your list. For example, if taking a deep breath helps you to relax, you may want to draw a picture of someone looking calm or meditating.

3. Make a collage of the pictures.

4. Under the picture, write "My Life Tools."

5. Date the picture.

6. Every few months, reflect back on the picture. Do you need to add to it? Or make a new picture?

7. For a twist on this activity, if you use Pinterest, you can create a board for your life tools. Add pins that reflect ways you reduce your emotional responses. Then, you'll have a reminder of your life tools on your phone, iPad, or computer when you might need them most.

What you may not know is that your brain can actually lie to you. It can leap to judgments and draw conclusions that aren't always accurate or rooted in fact. Mindfulness and learning to discern when your thoughts are incorrect or incomplete can often help in combating this, enabling you to slow your reaction and quell the negative self-chatter.

The first step is learning to listen to and discern your self-talk. Tool #6 from Chapter 9, Is It True?, provides some great tips to assist you with your discernment.

Take a moment to complete the Mindful Discernment worksheet to learn how to evaluate how you speak to yourself and reframe your words into positive actions or reminders.

By learning to be mindful of your actions and internal dialogue, as well as reinforcing healthy habits and coping strategies, you can achieve emotional equilibrium more often than not—something very useful on your journey of self-discovery.

The Girl Guide

Worksheet #18

Mindful Discernment

Directions: Using the Is It True? technique you've previously learned, make a list of the internal messages you tell yourself. Then, look for any outside evidence to support or replace the message. Finally, plan out your new motto to keep in mind or steps for changing your negative self-talk.

Self-Talk	True?	New Message or Plan
I am stupid.	No—I am earning average grades.	I am smart and capable.

Note to Self:
Don't Compare and Other Pointers

I would like to share with you my points for a happy and successful life:

» *Don't compare yourself to others, it's pointless. What other people's lives look like from the outside is seldom reality.*

» *Show appreciation and gratitude for every person in your life.*

» *Choose friends who will help you grow and tell you the truth.*

» *Never give up—'nuff said.*

» *An attractive woman is a strong and intelligent woman.*

» *Try to see the best in people.*

» *Have confidence in your dreams.*

» *Ignore the haters.*

There you go, my success tips! —Paula Earl

It happens to the best of us from time to time—we get overwhelmed. It's just part of being human. Fortunately, you are developing the tools necessary to reduce the frequency of those moments, and enable you to regain your equilibrium much sooner. Go back through the chapter and reflect on the scenario and the exercises included. Then take a moment to answer the reflection questions that follow.

My Voice

Keeping in mind the authentic you inside, answer the following:

▶ What makes me lose control? How long does it take me to recover?

▶ Do I have a coping plan to help me when I get overwhelmed? How effective is it?

▶ Do I remember to review the activities in this book regularly to hone my skills and reduce my outbursts? Why or why not?

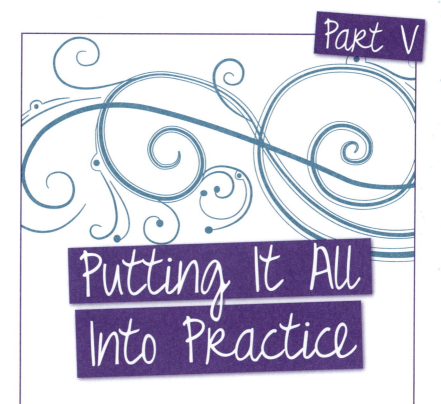

Part V

Putting It All Into Practice

The first 12 chapters of this book gave you everything you need to develop your own voice and face some of life's challenges. This next section helps you put it all into practice. Over the next 6 chapters, you'll learn about bullying, social networking, underperformance, perfectionism, developing a strong relationship with all of the "moms" in your life, and developing your talents. The pages are packed with tools, worksheets, and activities to help guide you toward your authentic self and build your resiliency.

But first, it's always good to think about some of life's more challenging situations. Take the quiz and see where you stand with regard to a few of life's adventures.

Quiz #5

Thinking About My Life

1. I know what to do if I am bullied.
   ☐ True   ☐ False

2. I tend to be a perfectionist when it comes to my studies.
   ☐ True   ☐ False

3. I don't always achieve my goals.
   ☐ True   ☐ False

4. I like to be online and have rules about being online that I've discussed with my parents.
   ☐ True   ☐ False

5. I take the time to explore my creative self and know my passions.
   ☐ True   ☐ False

Come back after you've tried a few of the activities to see if any of your answers have changed.

Chapter 13

Bouncing Back From Bullying

> *I remember being in middle school and being ignored by a group of girls that were my friends since second grade. All of a sudden they acted like I didn't exist. It hurt. A lot. I can still remember everything about that feeling.* —Sun, age 17

Bullying is something most of you will face in your lifetime. Recent statistics suggest that more than 70% of teens will face some form of bullying, including cyberbullying, relational aggression, and verbal bullying, at some point in their adolescence. Understanding what a bully is and what to do if you witness or are a victim of bullying is vital.

To get us thinking about this topic, I want you to read the following scenario and think about what you would do.

What Would You Do?

You are walking around the mall one day with a few friends when you see a group of girls taunting another girl. The person being taunted is clearly bothered by what is happening, but the girls tossing out the verbal taunts don't stop. In fact, the more upset the girl gets, the more the other girls continue the barrage of negative comments.

What do you do? Walk away because you don't want to get involved? Tell the girls to stop? Befriend the victim? Tell an adult?

Take a moment and write down what you would do in this case of taunting.

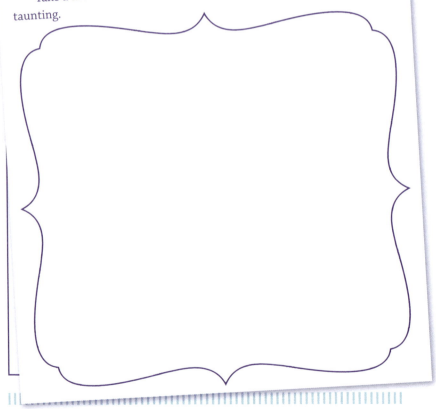

What Is Bullying?

Bullies come in all shapes and sizes, and the impact of their deeds is far reaching. Before I launch into a conversation about how to deal with the various types of bullying that exist, I think it's best to talk about what a bully is and what it isn't.

Law enforcement uses three basic questions to help determine whether or not a specific act falls within the legal definition of bullying:

- Does the perpetrator have some measure of power over the victim?
- Has some form of aggression—physical or emotional—occurred?
- Does the victim believe the acts of aggression will continue?

If you can answer "yes" to these questions, the event, whatever it was, will likely meet the legal definition of bullying.

There are three typical ways in which someone can be bullied: physical, verbal, and relational. Physical bullying includes all forms of physical aggression, as well as property destruction, and is what most people think of when they think of bullying. It is the most overt form of bullying, but accounts for less than half of all bullying. It is typically male-on-male, although there has been a recent rise in female-on-female physical bullying as girls are becoming more socialized toward aggression.

Verbal bullying refers to taunting, gossiping, name-calling, and, in the more extreme version, cyberbullying. It is the most common type of bullying and accounts for the majority of cases.

Although most people think of verbal bullying as being mostly girl-to-girl, it is actually perpetrated by both girls and boys.

Relational aggression is the most covert form of bullying and the most damaging. Typically girl-to-girl, this type of bullying attacks relationships through isolation, seclusion, shunning, and exclusion. Relational aggression is very difficult to detect as it can involve something as subtle as a particular rolling of eyes or hostile body language. Sure, that may sound like nothing, but to the victim, it feels as though you have been punched in the gut. Like the other forms of bullying, relational aggression undermines the victim's self-esteem and feeling of safety.

Tool #8

Bullying 101

The types of bullying include:

- ▸ **Physical**—Overt; involving physical acts of aggressions including hitting, shoving, kicking, and property destruction.
- ▸ **Verbal**—Typically the first type of bullying encountered; includes taunting, gossiping, name-calling, and cyber-bullying. Often a "gateway" to more aggressive forms of bullying.
- ▸ **Relational**—Covert; typically girl-to-girl; involves an attack on relationships; includes seclusion, exclusion, and shunning.

Now that you have a working understanding of what the definitions of bullying are, let's take a moment to talk about teasing and taunting.

Teasing is a normal part of growing up. Sometimes called banter or harmless fun, teasing is not meant to hurt. It is a normal exchange between people meant to generate laughter. It's innocent and shouldn't hurt.

But sometimes teasing goes too far and turns into taunting. Whenever someone is hurt by teasing, it is a sign that a boundary has been violated and the teasing needs to end. When that sign is further ignored, or when the point of the teasing is not an innocent exchange between people, but a one-sided attack that increases when the person being teased is upset—that is not teasing. That is taunting. And it's a type of bullying.

Dos and Don'ts of Getting Involved

Now that you have a strong understanding of the legal definition and types of bullying, what can you do about it, whether you are a witness or a victim?

First off, remember that no one has the power to diminish you without your permission. Part of the reason bullying, especially the relational type, works is because you feel powerless to do anything about it. You are left feeling hopeless and without friends—something that can eat away at your resiliency and leave you emotionally damaged. It does get better, see Tool #10 for help.

The good news is that you can do something about it. You can choose not to let the behavior of the bully destroy you. The various activities, worksheets, and tools provided throughout this book have all enabled you to develop many of your internal coping skills. You have learned that you only have control over yourself and your feelings. You know that although someone may do something that is very hurtful to you, you can choose to rise above it, even though that is a hard thing to do in the case of bullying.

On these pages, you have also learned how to deal with your emotions, how to develop a good sense of self, and how to focus on things you are grateful for. All of these skills will help you combat the more negative impacts of bullying. They will also help you to develop the perspective needed to avoid becoming a bully.

There is something else you can do as a witness or victim to help prevent the spread of bullying—report it. See Tool #9 for help.

Bullies continue to bully because there is a code of silence around bullying—most witnesses are afraid to get involved, and most victims are ashamed. Sure, it can be very hard to report acts of bullying. But when you don't speak out, your silence says the actions of the bully are acceptable to you. That what she is doing is okay. And it is never okay.

So learn what it means to bully. Make sure you do not hurt someone else in that way. And if you see acts of bullying, or if you are bullied, know who you can talk to and how you can help. By taking control, you can stop a bully's impact.

21st-Century Bullying

Technology is an amazing thing. In my lifetime, I've seen knowledge spread and grow at an amazing rate. You can Google almost anything, find out information in a nanosecond, connect with people in other places of the globe, and learn anything you can imagine. The development of the cell phone, Internet, and social networking has forever changed how we connect, interact, and find information. It is both exciting and a bit intimidating.

Bullying has taken a new look with the digital age. Cyberbullying, or acts of verbal and relational aggression that occur online or through technology, is on the rise. Some statistics report that more than 75% of all teens will experience some form of bullying through digital mediums including online and via texting.

Dos and Don'ts of Getting Involved

- ▶ DO know the difference between bullying and teasing.
- ▶ DON'T stay silent if you are feeling bullied. Tell an adult.
- ▶ DO report acts of bullying when you see them.
- ▶ DON'T avoid telling because of fear or shame.
- ▶ DO practice how you would tell an adult about bullying.
- ▶ DON'T allow bullying to continue.
- ▶ DO remember that the victim is never to blame.
- ▶ DON'T side with the bully.
- ▶ DO remember that it will get better.
- ▶ DON'T become a bully.

Cyberbullying typically includes verbal taunts and threats and works similar to verbal bullying and relational aggression. It also includes sexting.

As children become adolescents, and teasing morphs into flirting, taunting can turn into sexual bullying. This occurs when flirting begins to violate boundaries, making the victim feel degraded and afraid. Sexual bullying can lead to sexting, or the unwanted advances of one person to another via text. Sexting also includes the spreading of sexually explicit rumors and pictures for the purposes of hurting another person.

As with the other forms of bullying, cyberbullying and sexting are about power and control over another person. But unlike the

Tool #10

It Gets Better

Being bullied is never an easy thing to endure. It may make you feel hurt, ashamed, and powerless. But it doesn't need to destroy your self-esteem. The following reminders can help you shift your focus if you are feeling the negative effects of bullying.

- You have no control over what the bully does, but you have control over what you feel about it.
- Find your voice, speak out. Don't settle for silence.
- Find the positives—you are stronger, more compassionate, and more empathetic because of your experiences.
- Take action—report the bully, advocate for those who are bullying, and make people aware of the situation.
- You are not alone. Don't suffer in silence and shame. Tell a trusted friend or adult. Seek help if you need it. You will survive this.

kind of bullying that happens on a school campus and may take a while to spread from person to person, cyberbullying can spread rumors and gossip in a matter of seconds across a larger group of people.

Combating cyberbullying, like combating all forms of bullying, involves notifying authorities when it happens, practicing safe habits online (which I will go into more detail about in Chapter 15), and remembering that you can have the ultimate control over your reactions and feelings about bullying. There is life after bullying, it does get better.

When Bullying Turns Violent

We have all heard about the cases of school violence and bullycide (suicide that results directly from an incidence of bullying) that have occurred over the past decade. In almost all of these cases, the perpetrator was someone who had been bullied. There are warning signs that you or a friend may become aggressive or suicidal in response to the humiliation and shame that comes with being bullied. More common signs include:

- substance abuse,
- threatening acts of violence and talking about suicide,
- sudden changes in behavior, and
- continual rejection.

Although none of these things *means* someone will turn to violence as a way to cope, they can point to that potential. If you or any of your friends are showing these warning signs, it is important to tell an adult right away. No one deserves to feel the humiliation and shame associated with acts of bullying. So, do your part to help prevent bullying—report it when you see it, don't engage in acts yourself, and be a good friend to those in need.

Note to Self: It Takes Courage to Be Unique

Don't be afraid to stand up for who you are and be a model of creativity for others. Even if they act like they don't care, they will remember that someone had the courage to stand up and be different. Have the courage to be yourself, no matter what. —Erin Hastedt

This has been a hard chapter, focusing on one of the sad realities facing most children and teens. But talking openly and honestly about the hard stuff, including bullying, is the best way to remove the shame and deal with the problem. Growing up is hard. Taking the long journey to authenticity is hard. But it does get easier.

Take a moment and reflect on the scenario at the beginning of the chapter as you complete the self-reflection questions below.

My Voice

Keeping in mind the authentic you inside, answer the following:

- How do I feel about the different types of bullying? Have I ever been the victim of bullying in the past?
- What can I do to protect myself against bullying, including cyberbullying?
- How can I help my friends if they are bullied?
- Do I know any bullies? Is there anything I can do to help them?
- Have I ever spoken with my parents about bullying? What was that conversation like?

Chapter 14

Underperformance, Perfectionism, and Other Academic Mysteries

> *I hate admitting my mistakes. Or admitting when I am stressed. Or even admitting when I am sad. But, the only way I can learn to control it is if I first admit to it.* —Maria, age 17

School can be a difficult place for some of you. And many times, the center of that difficulty lies in academic problems. Some of you may struggle with motivation to get your homework completed or to study for tests, resulting in grades that are not as good as you would like them to be. Others of you may struggle with perfectionism, refusing to turn work in until it meets your exacting standards, also resulting in grades that are less than you would like. Either way, achieving less than you are capable of serves no one, least of all you.

In this chapter, you will explore some of the more common reasons girls struggle in school and how to combat them. But first, take a look at the following scenario and ponder what you might do in the same situation.

What Would You Do?

You used to love school, especially in the fifth and sixth grades. Things came pretty easy to you and being successful at school was looked at in a positive light by your peers. And then you started junior high . . .

No one looks at you positively when you earn good grades now. At least, no one you care about. All of your friends, and more importantly, the boy you like, think earning good grades makes you a "goody-goody."

So you stop turning in all of your work. You study a little less, and hang out online after school at little more. Your social life is certainly benefiting from the change of focus. But not your grades. And not your relationship with your parents. You've been careful not to let things slip too badly, but in truth, you are struggling with your poor grades as much as your parents are. You want to go back to being a straight-A student, but you want to hold on to your new set of friends too.

What do you do? Try to manage the social scene and make up your grades? Tell your teachers not to call on you so you can "fake dumb" in class? Tell your parents what's going on and ask for help? Just stick with the popularity thing because it means more to you right now anyway?

Take a moment and write down what you would do to navigate through the grade game.

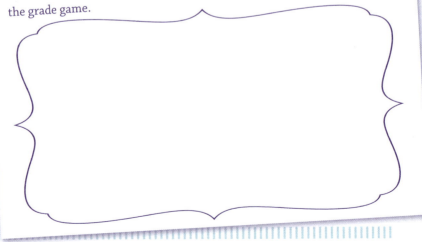

My School Feels Good to Me . . . Not

Ah yes, school. No matter whether you like it or hate it, school is part of your world. A large part. For some of you, you thrive on the social and academic dynamics of school. Some of you may like one aspect or another, and still others of you will hate the entire scene.

But what is it that can make school so hard? The workload and pressure? The social dynamics and expectations? The environment? In truth, all of these aspects can be a reason why some of you may find school difficult.

In order to change your performance at school, you are going to need to be willing to take a hard look at why it is difficult for you in the first place. You will need to look at your skills compared to the work required, your feelings about the social aspects of school, and your connections to the teachers and other staff. These things can all help you isolate why school is or is not a comfortable place.

Take a look at the My School and Me worksheet and use it as a guide to isolate the positive things you feel about school, as well as the more challenging things.

Once you have identified what is positive and not-so-positive about school, you can begin to develop a plan for dealing with the less-comfortable aspects of school. School performance, and underperformance, can often relate to issues of comfort within the environment as much as it can relate to your ability to do the work and deal with homework. So take some time to look at your comfort levels and connectedness to the school environment. Getting clear in this aspect of school can help you discern between

Worksheet #19: My School and Me

Directions: For each of the areas identified, indicate something positive and something you find challenging. Add additional aspects about school or other settings as appropriate for your life.

School Attribute	Something Good	Something Difficult
My teachers	I feel like my teachers care about the students.	Sometimes they don't seem to have enough time to make sure I understand things.
Homework		
Clubs		
Principal(s)		
Counselor(s)		
Friends		
Social Scene		
Lunch		

Now, take a moment and write a few words or sentences to describe how your school feels to you overall. What things are fabulous? What do you struggle with?

problems you can control and impact (like how you feel regarding school), and problems that will likely require more assistance from the educational staff (like problems related to skill mastery).

Getting a good education is important and vital to helping you as you make this journey of self-discovery. It's your job to be open enough with yourself to admit whatever problems you may be having, identify your personal barriers, and take steps toward helping to solve the problem.

I will show you some specific ways to address homework and test-taking challenges at the end of the chapter. But first, let's look at perfectionism and some of the unfortunate and, sadly, typical things that sometimes happen to girls regarding school as they enter early adolescence.

The Pressure Cooker

As we stated earlier, the first aspect of school that can cause some performance issues is related to the overall environment and comfort levels. The next aspect is the curriculum and your perceptions of academic performance and what that means. Some of you associate performance with being perfect. In other words, you've failed if you aren't perfect. And in that push to be perfect, you've managed turn school into a massive pressure cooker!

Now let me start by saying pressure and perfectionism are not necessarily bad things. In truth, they can be huge motivators. A certain amount of pressure is what will often motivate you to act, to achieve. Without it, most of you would lack the drive necessary for forward momentum. And without a little touch of perfectionism, you may never push yourself beyond your comfort levels.

> *I hate that I constantly feel stressed out about school. At the same time, I can't image things another way. The truth is, I will always push myself. It's just the way I am.* —Fabiana, age 17

But there is a negative aspect to pressure too. When the pressure gets too high, when it overwhelms your coping system, as in the case of perfectionism, it can keep you from taking risks or making mistakes. Perfectionism in the extreme can exert enough pressure to paralyze you and keep you from truly learning.

So how do you balance the pressures you face to ensure forward momentum and prevent paralysis? The answer lies in awareness, discernment, and honesty. Take a look at the next tool for practical guidelines to assist you in beating the trap of perfectionism.

Tool #11

Avoiding the Perfectionism Trap

- ▶ Acknowledge any problem you are having.
- ▶ Practice setting realistic goals.
- ▶ Focus on the process, not the outcome, but be willing to adjust the process as needed to get your desired outcome.
- ▶ Manage your perspective.
- ▶ Be honest with yourself.

Like everything else you have already learned in this book, combating the negative aspects of perfectionism happens when you take a balanced approach to your life and appropriately discern the truth in your environment. Perfectionism and pressure that rises to unhealthy levels often happen when you misperceive the environment and your performance. Take a look at Tool #12 and use it anytime you begin to feel your stress response kicking in.

Tool #12

Reflection

If you are struggling with perfectionism, even after reviewing the suggestions in Tool #11, try these questions as a way to help you refocus and reduce the negative aspects of perfectionism:

- Is my goal realistic? Am I expecting too much?
- What would happen if I failed?
- Am I being realistic?

Asking these questions and adjusting your expectations is the first step toward managing any perfectionistic behaviors.

Plan Ahead or Go Behind

I grew up with the saying "Plan ahead or go behind." It was my grandmother's way of making sure I understood the importance of having a plan and working toward my plan. In Chapter 8, you learned all about the importance of making plans and back-up plans in order to reach your goals. This is particularly true when it comes to school, homework, and test taking. Think of the following situation:

> You come home after a rough day and notice that your favorite show is on TV. You know your parents won't let you watch anything until your homework is completed. What are you going to do?
>
> You glance over the work and decide that you really don't have too much to do. Figuring you'll get it done on the way to school, you tell your parents the work is done and watch your show. But you forget to get it done in the morning. And you forget that you have tests in two classes.

Oops. Definitely a bad plan. One made worse because you didn't write down your assignments, lied to your parents, and didn't account for the time you actually needed to get your work finished.

Next time, you need a better plan, one that helps you remember to get everything written down so you know what you need to work on, and one that allows you the correct time to get things done. Take a moment and complete the My Homework Plan worksheet. By developing good habits regarding work completion and studying and prioritizing your work, you are making school and your education a strong focus. And that will keep you on the path toward your dreams.

Having a good plan to get your work done is great. But what happens if you get home and realize you are unclear as to *how* to complete your work. What then?

The easiest solution is to review your workload before leaving each class. Take a couple of minutes before the bell rings and you go home for the day to review your homework plan for the night. Make certain you understand everything you need to do and

The Girl Guide
Worksheet #20: My Homework Plan

Directions: Write down your assignments every night, including any tests, projects, chores, or extracurricular activities. Decide which order you will complete them and cross off each item as it is completed. If it is to be completed over several nights, add it to each plan for each night until it is due. When you are finished, put the homework in your backpack and get ready for the next day.

DAY 1

Class	Assignment	Due Date/Priority
Science	Lab sheet	Due on Friday; low priority

DAY 2

Class	Assignment	Due Date/Priority

DAY 3

Class	Assignment	Due Date/Priority

»

DAY 4

Class	Assignment	Due Date/Priority

DAY 5

Class	Assignment	Due Date/Priority

what's expected (see the next tool for help with this). And if you are unsure in any way, ask the teacher. That is why your teachers are there!

Understanding My Homework

Before leaving school, read each statement and decide whether or not it is true for you. For every "N" answer, make sure you find the missing information before you leave school.

Y or N   I have written down every assignment, including projects and tests.

Y or N   I know when every assignment is due.

Y or N   I know exactly what I must do for each task.

Y or N   I know how the work is being graded and what is expected.

Note to Self: Love Yourself First

Don't ever let anyone treat you like you're less than you are—even yourself. If you don't like yourself, other people won't either. Only the people who matter in your life, the ones you respect and value, should have any influence on how you choose to conduct yourself. Be yourself. You are going to have to live with yourself for an awfully long time, so make sure who you are is someone you like. —B. E. Sanderson

In this chapter, you have shifted your focus to school performance. You've looked at the things that are comfortable for you about school, as well as the things that are not so comfortable. And you've learned how to develop a plan for getting your work finished.

The planning tools you've learned can be used not only with work completed in school, but with the goals you developed at the beginning of the book, as well as anything that may take a little planning to execute. Take a moment and reflect on the things you've learned about performance in this chapter as you complete the self-reflection questions below.

My Voice

Keeping in mind the authentic you inside, answer the following:

- ▶ What things are hard for you in school? Have you made a plan to deal with the harder things? How comfortable are you with that plan?
- ▶ Are there aspects of your life where you are a bit of a perfectionist? What are the positive aspects of perfectionism? The negative aspects?
- ▶ Did you go through this chapter and devise a plan to deal with homework and task completion? Why or why not?
- ▶ If you did develop a homework plan, what are going to be the hardest aspects of the plan to actually execute? What can you do to make it a little easier?

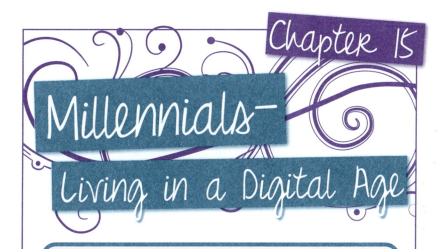

Chapter 15

Millennials—
Living in a Digital Age

> I can't imagine being without my phone. I mean, I text my friends, go onto my Facebook account, watch YouTube videos, and read books on my Kindle app. I can do anything on my phone. —Sonji, age 15

Have you ever seen the commercial where a young teen is speaking to her younger siblings and telling them how easy they have it because technology has changed to allow them to move their TVs anywhere in the house? That commercial pretty much sums up what it means to be alive today. Technology and information is growing at such a fast rate that millions of new ideas occur every second. The things that are around today will be eclipsed with more new things in a matter of days and weeks.

One of the more recent changes brought about by technology is the whole concept of social networking. And with the host of positives that can be created with the increased knowledge and technology come some risks and the potential for new areas of danger.

But before we get into all of that, take a minute and read over the following scenario.

What Would You Do?

Your friends are all about technology. They have phones and Facebook accounts and basically live online. You aren't allowed to have a Facebook account yet. You don't have your own e-mail account. And you don't even have a phone. You want to plead your case to your parents as to why you need to step into the digital age, but you don't know what you can say or how you should say it.

Take a moment and write down a conversation between you and your parents. Remember to think of all of the reasons they aren't ready to let you jump into social networking, and your reasons for requesting that they do. (If you do have a phone and social networking accounts already, step into the shoes of someone your age who doesn't and imagine how you might approach your reluctant parents with the idea.)

The Digital Age

It's an exciting time to be alive. Within the last decade alone, technology has boomed, bringing us a new level of techno-gadgetry for our homes and our lives. Just look at the following list of things that have become commonplace in many homes and lives in the last 10 years:

- flat panel TVs,
- HDTVs and DVRs,
- eReaders,
- iPads and tablets,
- smartphones,
- bluetooth technology,
- high-speed Internet connections and WiFi,
- online social networking and gaming,
- social media sites,
- print on demand books, and
- flash storage.

These items were nothing more than something cool in a sci-fi movie a few decades ago. And now, they're commonplace in many parts of the world.

The technological advances don't stop there. In the past year alone, there have quantum leaps in almost every industry. Some of the bigger leaps include the following:

- nanotech and nanorobotics,
- CPUs with the ability to learn and develop new synapses like the human brain,
- alternative sources of energy and improved batteries,
- increased use of optics and photonics,

▶ changes in genonomics including the prevention of genetically born diseases, and

▶ humanoid robotics.

Although the technology is incredible, so are the risks as the information and technology increases faster than our ethics. Never before have we been less able to predict the future. And never before has it been more important that we learn to think about and creatively approach problems.

Your generation will lead the way into this new era of information. And your generation will come face-to-face with the new dangers that have emerged, including identity theft, cyberbullying, and sexting, to name a few.

So how do you enjoy the benefits of the increased information and technology while also protecting yourself? The next two sections will look at the realities of social networking, as well as keeping yourself safe online. Before we get started, I want you to complete the My Life Online worksheet and take a look at the places you frequent online and your Internet savvy.

Facebook, YouTube, and Texting, Oh My

The social networking scene is nothing new for teens. Most of you have a phone with texting capabilities, the ability to chat online, and access to Facebook, YouTube, and other online sites. Some of you may be online gamers, loving World of Warcraft and similar games. Those of you who may not have easy access to the Internet have probably figured out how to use your gaming systems to access sites online. Even most televisions enable Internet

Directions: Take a moment to think about how you spend you time online and then answer the following questions:

1. Which sites do you visit most often? Why?

2. Do your parents know your passwords? Why or why not?

3. Do you have e-mail? Do your parents have access to your accounts?

4. Do you text? Do your parents monitor your texts?

I asked a lot of questions about your parents and how closely they monitor you online. How do you feel about them having access to your accounts? Does it bother you? Why or why not?

usage now. You Google answers to homework questions, stream movies and music on your tablets, and read books on your phones.

Social networking and access to the Web are good things for the most part. But as I mentioned earlier, social networking does have a downside, including the ability to completely take over your life.

> *What? Give up my phone and Kindle? Not gonna happen. Not ever.*
> —Sarah, age 13

As we get started, take a moment to isolate how often you use some form of social networking and the Internet. Keep a little pad with you and jot down every time you text, e-mail, chat, or go online. Do this a couple of hours every day for a week. Then complete the My Online Habits worksheet and take a real look at your Internet and social networking habits.

As you completed the worksheet, what did you notice? Are you online more or less often than you thought? Do you predominately use social networking as something more educational or more social? Do you use texting and chatting as a replacement for in-person conversations?

The answers to these questions can shine a light on the value you place on social networking in your life, and whether or not it is mostly positive or negative for you. Psychologists are just beginning to study the impact of social media on people, but the early research indicates that social media, including texting; chatting; and Facebook, Twitter, YouTube, and similar sites, can be *more addicting* than alcohol and smoking. That's right—I said, "more addicting"! This is even truer for people who struggle with self-esteem is-

My Online Habits

Directions: Use this form to keep track of your technology use for a few days. Include e-mail, text, chat, and Internet usage.

E-mail, chat, text, or Internet (include site)?	Purpose	Date/Time
Text	Chat with friends	Today, 18 texts

Now, take a moment to reflect on your usage. Do you see any patterns? Any concerns? Jot down your thoughts here.

sues and for introverts who find social networking so much easier than developing relationships in person.

Once you've looked at your online habits, take a look at the following tool to help you balance the positives of social media with the risks.

Online Balancing Act

- ⮊ Cultivate relationships in person, as well as online.
- ⮊ Never text and drive.
- ⮊ Turn off your mobile device and computer at night.
- ⮊ If you find yourself almost obsessed with social media sites, it's time for a social media break.
- ⮊ "Unplug" from the Internet one day a month.
- ⮊ Leave your phone upstairs in your room one day a week during dinner or hide it in the very bottom of your backpack when having lunch with your friends. See how not having easy access to your device changes the way you interact with others. How does it make you feel when others around you are plugged in and you're wanting their attention?

Being Safe Online

As I mentioned earlier in this chapter, there are positive and negatives about living in the digital age. In addition to the addiction risks mentioned above, other dangers including everything from identity theft, to online predators, to texting while driving.

Fortunately, keeping yourself safe is really just about forming a few good habits and maintaining them throughout your life. These habits are just like the boundaries you learned to set earlier in the book and are designed to help you minimize risk and keep yourself safe.

Before I jump into the habits, let's review a few basic realities about being online. First, get rid of your assumption of privacy online. Pretty much anything you put out there has the potential of being stolen, misused, or hacked, no matter how secure your privacy settings. With sensitive information, like banking or financial information, you may have some amount of recourse. But most of the time you will not. So be careful what you disclose online. Things related to your identity like your social security number, your driver's license number, and personal contact information should not be given out in most cases. You want to keep these things private.

Which brings me to what you say online . . .

Have you ever been on Facebook or YouTube and read through the various posts or comments? Have you then wondered, "Dude! You actually said that?" Yeah, I have. See, anyone and everyone can read those posts, including a teacher, prospective boss, college recruiter, or your crush's parents. And many times, they do. So, the next time you are frustrated and ready to fire off a comment or post, stop and think, "Am I okay with a college recruiter reading this?" The same thinking applies to posting photos and other information you may be tempted to share. The Internet is not private. Not by any stretch. Just imagine how disastrous it could be to lose an important scholarship or place at the competitive school of your dreams because of something silly you posted one time—it has happened!

Another important thing to remember is deleting something doesn't really make it go away online. There will always be an echo of the post, the photo, whatever it is you added. That "echo" can be hacked into and spread around. So again, think before you post.

Finally, a few words about privacy settings. Privacy settings on places like YouTube and Facebook won't guarantee your safety, especially if you don't adjust them periodically. Take Facebook, for example. Did you know that a friend of a friend can view your posts unless you set your privacy settings to prevent that? The same applies to pictures and videos you share. It is important to think about this as you get online and set up accounts.

There are several things you can do to keep yourself safe. Take a look at the Safety Online tool. You may want to copy this and post it near the computer or in your room as a reminder.

Tool #15

Safety Online

- ⇥ Change your passwords regularly, every 6 months at the longest.
- ⇥ Never give out personal information online.
- ⇥ Remember, nothing online is really private.
- ⇥ Not everyone is who he says he is online.
- ⇥ Stay away from cyberbullying.
- ⇥ Let your parents or a trusted adult know if you are being harassed in any way online.
- ⇥ Give your parents access to your online accounts.

I've spent the bulk of this section talking about social media etiquette and safety. But I would be remiss if I didn't mention texting and driving. You know you shouldn't do it. You know there are laws against it. And you all know someone who still texts and drives. So here's the real deal—the National Traffic Safety Administration reports that traffic accidents are the leading cause of fatalities among teens. And distracted driving is the cause of many of those accidents. What's more, according to the Centers for Disease Control, more than 32% of teens admit to texting or e-mailing while driving—a leading cause of distracted driving.

Bottom line, texting and driving is dangerous. So don't do it. Ever. When you learn to drive, take your phone and put it in your purse. Keep it out of site. Period.

This chapter was all about social networking and what it means to live in this age of technology. As you read the Note to Self and move into the self-reflection questions, I want you to think about why social media is such a huge part of your life. My guess is that it relates to the need to connect we talked about in Section II of the book. And as important as the connections are, you are still the first and most important relationship you will make. Take as much time to develop your relationship with yourself as you do your online relationships. That is what will help you the most on the path toward authenticity.

> # Note to Self: Your BFF Is You
>
> *If I could give you one piece of advice for life, it would be not to be afraid to be friends with yourself. Wherever you go and whatever you do, you will be the one person who will be right with you the whole way, and you can either view this person as an enemy or a friend. Pay attention to how you talk to yourself, and spend at least as much time encouraging yourself and giving yourself pep talks as you do criticizing yourself.*
>
> *Being your own friend doesn't make you selfish, and you don't have to be a perfect person to like yourself. In fact, understanding your strengths and weaknesses and accepting them all can be one of the most freeing decisions you can make and can actually help you meet your goals. If you like yourself just as you are, even as you change from year to year, being always curious about the person you are and are becoming, you really can have a supportive friend for life.* —Lisa Rivero

You are part of the Millennials, the generation that has embraced technology in a way previous generations never considered. For you, streaming videos, texting friends, and reading eBooks is the norm. You have redefined what it means to interact with media. It is an exciting time. But like anything, it comes with new and substantial threats.

This chapter has been all about exploring the benefits and risks of a digital age. The worksheets, tools, and activities have all been developed to help you reap the best this age has to offer, while managing the risk. Take a moment to go back through the chapter and complete whatever journal entries you may have skipped. Then come back and reflect on the following questions.

My Voice

Keeping in mind the authentic you inside, answer the following:

- ▶ What social media venues are you a part of? How often are you on the sites?
- ▶ How would you feel if you couldn't text, chat, or go online for 24 hours?
- ▶ What is the best use of technology you've participated in over the last year? Why was it the best?
- ▶ What dangers are you aware of online? How do you deal with them?
- ▶ Do you feel you can trust the people you meet online? Why or why not?
- ▶ What are the rules regarding technology in your house? Do you agree with them?
- ▶ How technologically savvy are your parents?
- ▶ Do your parents know your passwords to your accounts? Do you think they should? Why or why not?

Chapter 16

The Mother-Daughter Connection

> *My mom says you have to be silent in order to listen. I hate to admit it, but I think she is right.* —Julie, age 13

Few relationships at home change more during adolescence than the mother-daughter relationship. Maybe you were close with your mother in elementary school, only to find yourself frustrated and at odds with her frequently now. Or maybe you've never had a close relationship and you feel like you need her more than ever as you enter your adolescence. And maybe you don't know your biological mom, but you do have a mother-daughter-like relationship with another adult female in your life.

Whatever may be true for you, the next few years can be fraught with a level of tension that is new as both you and your mom try to adapt to the changing reality of who you are now.

Before we get into some of the more typical stumbling blocks you two may face as you make your way toward adulthood, read over the scenario that follows and think about how you might handle the situation.

What Would You Do?

Your mom is the best! She volunteered with your teacher in elementary school, went on the field trips, and always made time for you each day. But recently, her need to connect with you is getting to be a bit stifling. She asks you about your day and your friends all of the time, tries to be "cool" whenever she is carpooling, and offers advice at the worst times. You love her and really appreciate everything she has done for you, but you need a little space.

What do you do? How do you tell her that you love her but need some breathing room? Should you even say anything?

Take a moment and write down what you would do to navigate through this changing relationship.

Changing Relationships

It's happened. You're entering the teen years. And with that, your needs and wants in terms of your relationship with your parents are changing. Especially when it comes to the relationship with your mom. You are walking that fine line between wanting a strong attachment to her and needing some separation. And you know what? Your mom is walking that same hard line, wanting to hold on to you before you run off and become an adult, yet also wanting to give you the space you need to grow. It is a recipe for tension and conflict. Not surprisingly, you may find yourself arguing more than you used to.

But does this stage of your life have to mean conflict? Are you hardwired to having some difficulties at this time of life?

In some ways, I think the answer is a resounding yes. You need distance in order to become your own person. But you also need attachments to feel safe enough to go out on your own. Tension and conflict is an inevitable result of the balancing act.

But this isn't necessarily a bad thing. And there are ways you can quell some of the frustration. Take a moment to work through the I Need You, But . . . worksheet. It will help give you some insight as to how you would like the relationship with your mom to grow and mature. When you are done, ask your mom to complete something similar and talk through it together.

Communication 101

Moms seem to have an answer for everything. When you were younger, her pieces of advice were like little pearls you strung

Worksheet #23: I Need You, But . . .

Directions: Take a moment and read each statement, indicating if you agree or disagree.

Things Mom Does (the Good and the Annoying)	Keep As Is	Change It (and How)
Comes in to tell me good night every night	Keep doing it, I like the connection	But don't get mad if I don't really want to talk

Now, take a moment and reflect on your relationship with your mom. Write down the ways in which you like being connected and the things that are hard for you in your relationship.

around your heart. Lately, they feel more like pieces of lead chaining you to a life you are dying to break free from. The advice now feels like a lecture—an endless lecture.

> *You know what my mom needs? A teen dictionary! That way she stops thinking I am always mad and begins to understand that I am just trying to find my voice.* —Elizza, age 15

Sometimes you may want to argue with your mom, insisting that she has no understanding of who you are and what you want. You try to calmly disagree with her and/or her ideas, but it seems to always end in an argument of epic proportions.

What do you do? How can you express your thoughts and opinions without it always turning into a fight? The answer lies in understanding and using a few of the tools already presented through the book, including taking ownership for your feelings and trying to understand your mom's perspective on things.

Additionally, there are a few typical roadblocks to communication that can get in the way of clear communication (see Tool #16). Being aware of these and what to do about them can go a long way to preventing the disagreements that come up between you and your mom from turning into epic battles.

Tool #16

Overcoming Communication Roadblocks

- ▶ Remain calm.
- ▶ Try to keep emotions out of the conversation.
- ▶ Clearly state what you want/need.
- ▶ Listen to what is being said.
- ▶ No blaming, shaming, or arguing.

Preparing for Flight

I mentioned earlier that the struggle between mother and daughter is really a battle between needing the security of an attachment to your mom and needing to branch out on your own. It is a normal struggle as you prepare to leave the house in a few years. And a very scary one. If your relationship with your mom has been pretty strong and healthy, with appropriate boundaries and a strong connection, the journey will be less rocky. But if you two have struggled with boundaries and connections, the journey may be fraught with even more volatility.

Regardless of which is true for you, there are some things you can do to help keep your mind centered on the aspects of your relationship with your mom that have been meaningful and helpful to you.

This next activity, My Mom, builds on the Friendship Cards and About Me Cards discussed in earlier chapters. Take a moment to complete the activity in your journal. Better yet, use the guidelines to make a movie for your mom. Both of you will enjoy it for years to come.

As I mentioned earlier, the changing dynamic in your relationship with your mom is really about detaching and becoming your own person. Fitting, given the journey of self-discovery you've been on throughout this entire book. Most psychologists agree that you can't ever really become your own person until you leave the house. And even then, you will struggle with that balance between being attached to your mom and being an independent woman. When my mom died not too long ago, I found myself going through that same struggle I did when I was a teen—trying to figure out who I was without my mom.

Take a moment and complete the Memories activity. Create a memory book of not just the things you and your mom have done together, but with pictures that represent the aspects of you—the authentic you—that have been influenced by your mom. For example, my need to create comes from my mom and my grandmother. It is a quality I see in both of my girls as well. Use this memory book as a reminder of all of the positive ways your mom has helped shape your life, even as you enter into a new and different kind of relationship with her.

Finally, take a moment to complete the Fun Things With Mom worksheet. As you grow and change, and as your relationship changes, it's more important than ever to carve out a little time together. But, the things you used to do together may not be things you want to do now. Take a moment and think about ways the two of you can still connect, both now and in a few years when you have left the house.

Activity #18

My Mom

Directions: Using the steps that follow, think about what makes your mom awesome.

1. Using your journal or something similar, list some of the things that remind you of your mom. Include those activities that you like to do together.

2. Find or draw pictures that reflect your list.

3. Make a collage of the pictures.

4. Under the collage, write something nice about your mom.

5. Date the page.

6. Every few months, reflect back on the page. Do you need to add to it? Or make a new picture?

7. For a twist on this activity, follow the guidelines and make a movie featuring photos of you and your mom with some of your favorite songs. This would make a great gift for her to show her you care!

Memories

Directions: Follow the steps below to help you create a set of unique memories of you and your mom.

1. Using your journal or something similar, list your favorite memories of your mom and/or the other influential women in your life.

2. Find or draw pictures to represent those memories.

3. Make a memory scrapbook with the pictures and other things that remind you of the wonderful times you have had.

4. Date the book.

5. Add to it as you form new memories.

6. Do this project with your mom—you will make even more fun memories this way. Together you could add new dimensions to the project, such as making a digital scrapbook using Photoshop, compiling some of your favorite recipes of the goodies you bake together into a cookbook with photos, or creating a soundtrack for your relationship right now.

Fun Things With Mom

Directions: Take some time to think about what you'd like to do with your mom and fill out the chart below.

Things I'd like to do with my mom	When I'd like to do them	Completed (Y or N)

Note to Self: Live Life for Yourself First

My Dear Daughter—Above all, I want you to be you. I want you to be with people who like you for who you are. I don't want you to ever think you need to change who you are in order to make someone like you. Anyone who wants you to do this isn't interested in the real you and isn't worth your time. Anyone who tells you "if you want to be my friend, you have to do this or this" isn't truly your friend. Any man who tells you "if you love me you'll do something you don't want to do" isn't worth your attention. You are truly wonderful, and I don't ever want you to tear yourself down in order to fit into a mold someone else thinks you should fit into. And I want you to be the type of person who does this for others. To be supporting and compromising and giving without losing any part of yourself. Bottom line, life is too short to live it for others. Be mindful of others, be kind and caring. But live your life for yourself. —Michelle McLean

Mothers and their daughters—it is one of the most complex relationships around. And one that has been studied since people first started studying how people connect. Your mother is your first and, some may say, most important connection you will forge. She can help you find a particular path, or show you which paths you want to avoid. She is someone you'll idolize and someone you may resist. Whatever your relationship is with her, she is likely one of the biggest influences you have ever had.

In this chapter, you looked at the ever-changing relationship with all of the "moms" in your life. You examined your communication style, how to connect as a young adult, and why you may find yourself in conflict.

Take a moment and reflect on the exercises throughout the chapter, as well as the reflection questions below.

My Voice

Keeping in mind the authentic you inside, answer the following:

- ▶ How would I describe my relationship with the moms in my life? Are there things about the relationships I would like to change in some way?
- ▶ What is the single most important thing I have learned from my mom so far?
- ▶ I will be leaving the house soon. What makes me most sad about leaving related to my mom?
- ▶ If I could tell my mom one thing, what would it be?
- ▶ Do I have any regrets related to my relationship with my mother? What are they?

Chapter 17

Developing Your Creative Self

> *I had a teacher that always made us find creative solutions to problems. It was the best thing I've ever learned.* —Anastasia, age 16

Most of you probably think of creativity as something related to the arts. In truth, being creative means much more. Creativity not only refers to the act of creating something, but also the ability to think divergently and find ways around conventionalism. In other words, creativity is a form of "out-of-the-box" problem solving.

Over the next chapter, you will learn how to tap into your creative self and explore nontraditional ways of looking at the world. It is a skill that will help you not only as you journey toward your authentic self, but in any endeavor.

In the next scenario, I want you to think of all of the creative ways you can answer the question posed and write them down.

What Would You Do?

Your teacher is into creative problem solving tasks. She tells your group to make a list of all of the things you can think of that are "red."

Make a list of those things.

Then she explains that there are many meanings of the word "red." Think of all of the other meanings there are for "red," like "I read a book" and any others you may think of, and continue your list.

How many did you come up with? Did you need guidance in order to broaden your thoughts to things other than the color "red"?

Creativity 101?

This entire book has been about finding your own unique point of view in the world. One of the best ways to do this is by stretching your creativity muscle. As I mentioned in the opening, being creative isn't limited to being artistic. Some of the most creative endeavors have happened in the science and math industries. Take some of the new technology I mentioned in Chapter 15, for example. Nanorobotics is definitely born of creativity. As was the computer Watson, made famous on the game show *Jeopardy!* a few years ago.

Stretching your creativity muscles enables you to approach problems as opportunities for new perspectives. It enables you to open your mind to new ideas and helps to create perspective. In the opening chapters of this book, I listed creativity as an important aspect of a healthy lifestyle. That is because creativity not only helps to develop your problem-solving skills and perspective taking, it opens you up to learning and allows an outlet to the emotions you have no doubt felt along this journey.

When you first started on this path of self-discovery, I said that you would need to be brave, have faith, and be fearless. The same attributes are needed when you embrace creativity. Additionally, dedicating yourself to a creative mindset will help you become more adventurous, develop your faith, and keep you on the path to your authentic self.

Take a look at the Being Creative worksheet and open your mind to the wealth of creative options you can find when you are willing to ask yourself "What if?" and "What else?"

The Girl Guide
Worksheet #25

Being Creative

Directions: Take a moment and think of all of the things you can do with the items or topics listed. Then add a few items and topics yourself.

Topics/Items	What I Can Do With Them	More Things I Can Do
Paperclips and note cards	Make a garland celebrating a holiday	Make an old-fashioned comic strip
Toothpicks and playdough		
Paperback books, empty paper towel rolls, and markers		
Things that are "blue"		

Many Paths

Creativity is not something you are born with exclusively. It is a way of looking at the world that opens you up to possibility. Developing creativity requires spending a little time every day exploring the world of "What if?" It means seeing obstacles as challenges and being willing to fail a hundred, a thousand, tens of thousands of times before figuring out a solution.

As I mentioned, developing creativity involves doing something creative daily. Take a look at the following list of spontaneous thinking games and activities used in programs like Odyssey of the Mind. These activities, along with brainteasers and Mensa puzzles, are designed to foster out-of-the-box thinking.

Tool #17

Embracing Creativity

Try to do as many of these open-ended activities as possible:
- Using only baby marshmallows, toothpicks, and notecards, build the biggest structure you can.
- Using spaghetti and gummy worms, make a bridge.
- Make a list of everything that can be "read." (*Hint:* Remember all of the definitions of the word!)
- Pretend you are on a deserted island with only three items. What are they and why do you have them?

Doing activities such as these stretch out your creative muscles. Do something creative every day!

Other ways to practice your creativity include the brain bender games available on most gaming systems and all over the Internet, as well as doing something as simple as asking "What if?" with various scenarios. For example, "what if" you had to get from home to school only making left turns. How would you do it? Or, "what if" tomorrow was speak-in-adjectives day. How could you tell me what you did without using anything but adjectives?

How you practice your creativity isn't nearly as important as developing the skills to try things without fear and to think divergently.

Problem Solving Revisited

You live in a world that measures everything in terms of testing. Most school districts focus on the high-stakes testing that is required nationally. And sometimes that focus doesn't promote creative thinking or advanced problem-solving skills. But, in life you will need both. And on the road toward your authentic self, you will need every tool you can get your hands on to foster divergent thinking.

Problem solving using creativity enables you to embrace solutions you may not have otherwise considered. Furthermore, such problem solving fosters risk-taking, collaboration, and self-reflection—attributes you have been working on throughout the book.

In Chapter 15, I mentioned that both knowledge and technology are increasing so fast we really don't know what the future is going to look like. I went on to mention that learning to think will be more important than ever. Creative problem solving is a great way to develop those thinking skills and prepare for an uncertain future. It requires brainstorming free from fear of making mistakes, as well as reflection, task analysis, and adaptation.

Approaching life from a creative point of view will give you the tools you need to overcome any obstacle. Additionally, creativity fosters adaptability, which can allow you to bend with life's punches, instead of being completely knocked out by them. Take a minute and review the goal setting you did at the beginning of this book. Using a little creativity, are there additional ways you could achieve some of the goals? Add to Worksheet #23 as needed to allow some additional creativity to enhance your problem-solving and goal-setting skills.

Note to Self: Be Yourself

Don't be afraid to be yourself.

I've always been kind of a spaz. When I was a kid, adults were always trying to rein me in, tell me to control my energy, lower my voice, don't be so crazy all of the time! I felt like I was wrong somehow. Not doing something wrong, but that I was actually just WRONG.

Then I grew up and embraced my inner spaz. It's who I am and I'm quite happy to admit it. I wish I'd been able to learn that lesson earlier. —Gretchen McNeil

This chapter was all about learning to look at problems with a creative eye. If you did the activities, you learned that the simple answer is not always the best answer. You learned to push out of your comfort zone, take risks, and how to brainstorm. These attributes are needed if you are going to continue your journey inward beyond the scope of this book, and learning these tasks can help you overcome any obstacle that you may encounter.

Take a moment to think about everything you have learned about yourself over the past few weeks. Then read and answer the questions below.

My Voice

Keeping in mind the authentic you inside, answer the following:

- Reflect back on a few of the problems you have encountered over the past month or so. Using your new creative skills, can you brainstorm other solutions? How do you think these new solutions may have worked?
- Sometimes it is scary to try new things and experiment with new ideas. Why is that? What can you do to combat that fear?
- Creativity requires a measure of risk—risk of failure, risk of humiliation, and other risks. How will you deal with these types of risks and be willing to continue the path of creativity?
- Reflect back on your dream poster and goals. Are there creative and nontraditional ways you can achieve some of those dreams?

Final Thoughts

We live in a noisy world, filled with distractions and other temptations, all designed to pull us from our goals and silence our voices. But it is an exciting time too. One filled with opportunities that other generations have not had. The trick is knowing how to be authentic, cultivate good habits, stay focused on your goals and dreams, and respect yourself and others. Hopefully some of the tools, activities, and stories in this book have been of some help.

My sincere wish for everyone reading this, whether a girl or her parent, is that the book becomes a springboard of conversation and a catalyst of growth. You are amazing just as you are. You have potential you are just beginning to realize. With the right tools and dedication, you can be more than you ever thought possible, simply by embracing the authentic you that lives inside.

As you grow and change, be sure to come back and revisit this book and the activities inside. Although they are simple, they are designed to put you in touch with sometimes silent parts of yourself and help you stay on track with your goal of being authentic and developing resiliency.

I'd love to hear from you as you make this journey. So, please, feel free to share your thoughts. You can reach me via e-mail at Christine@christinefonseca.com or find me on my many social networking sites.

Until then, I wish you all the best on your journey toward yourself.

Recommended Resources

The Girl Guide covers a wide range of topics as it goes through the skills and tools needed when you make that journey toward your authentic self. But there are so many things still to discuss. It is merely the beginning.

The recommended readings provide more information on empowerment, bullying, stress, mental health concerns, and risky behaviors.

Empowerment and Inspiration

Sometimes you just need a little inspiration and guidance. The following books are filled with advice, strategies, and stories that inspire:

- *The Struggle to Be Strong: True Stories by Teens About Overcoming Tough Times* edited by Al Desetta and Sybil Wolin
- *The Girls' Book of Wisdom: Empowering, Inspirational Quotes From Over 400 Fabulous Females* edited by Catherine Dee
- *Help Yourself for Teens: Real-Life Advice for Real-Life Challenges* by Dave Pelzer
- *Chocolate for a Teen's Soul: Life-Changing Stories for Young Women About Growing Wise and Growing Strong* by Kay Allenbaugh

Stress, Anxiety, and Depression

Girls and emotions go hand in hand at any age, especially during adolescence. The following books offer practical advice for dealing with everything from anxiety and stress to depression:

- *Dealing With the Stuff That Makes Life Tough: The 10 Things That Stress Girls Out and How to Cope With Them* by Jill Zimmerman Rutledge
- *Smart Teens' Guide to Living With Intensity: How to Get More Out of Life and Learning* by Lisa Rivero
- *The Stress Reduction Workbook for Teens: Mindfulness Skills to Help You Deal With Stress* by Gina M. Biegel
- *The Anxiety Workbook for Teens: Activities to Help You Deal With Anxiety and Worry* by Lisa M. Schab
- *Beyond the Blues: A Workbook to Help Teens Overcome Depression* by Lisa M. Schab

Dealing With the Hard Stuff

The teen years are often characterized with risky choices and hard decisions. The following books can help with everything from the evolving mother-daughter relationship, to relationships and dating, to bullying and more:

- *The Truth About Dating, Love, and Just Being Friends* by Chad Eastham
- *Teen Love: On Relationships: A Book for Teenagers* by Kimberly Kirberger
- *In Love and in Danger: A Teen's Guide to Breaking Free of Abusive Relationships* by Barrie Levy
- *Between Mother and Daughter: A Teenager and Her Mom Share the Secrets of a Strong Relationship* by Judy Ford and Amanda Ford
- *Girl Wars: 12 Strategies That Will End Female Bullying* by Cheryl Dellasega and Charisse Nixon

References

Beck, A. T., & Steer, R. A. (1993). *Manual for the Beck Anxiety Inventory.* San Antonio, TX: Harcourt Assessment.

Brooks, R., & Goldstein, S. (2001). *Raising resilient children: Fostering strength, hope, and optimism in your child.* New York, NY: Contemporary Books.

Centers for Disease Control and Prevention. (2012). Youth risk behavior surveillance—United States, 2011. *MMWR, 61*(4), 6.

Cook, M. (1999). *Effective coaching.* New York, NY: McGraw Hill.

Covey, S. (1998). *The seven habits of highly effective teens.* New York, NY: Fireside.

Eisenberg, N., Spinard, T. L., Fabes, R. S., Reiser, M., Cumberland, A., Shepard, S. A., . . . & Thompson, M. (2004). The relations of effortful control and impulsivity to children's resiliency and adjustment. *Child Development, 75,* 25–46.

Mueller, C. (2009). Protective factors as barriers to depression in gifted and nongifted adolescents. *Gifted Child Quarterly, 53,* 3–14. Abstract retrieved from http://gcq.sagepub.com/cgi/content/abstract/53/1/3

Pipher, M. (1994). *Reviving Ophelia: Saving the selves of adolescent girls.* New York, NY: Ballantine Books.

Prince-Embury, S. (2007, 2006). *Resiliency Scales for Children & Adolescents: A profile of personal strengths manual.* San Antonio, TX: Harcourt Assessment.

Simmons, R. (2002). *Odd girl out: The hidden culture of aggression in girls.* Orlando, FL: Harcourt.

Vannest, K., Reynolds, C., & Kamphaus, R. (2008). *BASC-2 intervention guide.* Bloomington, MN: Pearson.

Wiseman, R. (2002). *Queen bees & wannabees: Helping your daughter survive cliques, gossip, boyfriends & other realities of adolescence.* New York, NY: Three Rivers Press.

About the Author

Critically acclaimed nonfiction and young adult fiction author **Christine Fonseca** believes that writing is a great way to explore humanity. Using her training and expertise as an educational psychologist, Christine is dedicated to helping children of all ages find their voice in the world. Her nonfiction titles include *Emotional Intensity in Gifted Students* and *101 Success Secrets for Gifted Kids* and delve into the often misunderstood world of giftedness and emotional intensity. In addition to her nonfiction titles, Christine is the author of several YA novels including the Gothic romances, *Lacrimosa* and *Libera Me* (from the Requiem Series), and a psychological thriller, *Transcend*.

When she's not writing or spending time with her family, she can be found sipping too many skinny vanilla lattes at her favorite coffee house or playing around on Facebook and Twitter. For more information about Christine or her books, visit her website (http://christinefonseca.com) or blog (http://christinefonseca. blogspot.com).

About the Contributors

I could not write a book for girls without taking a moment to introduce you to the two women who shaped so much of my life—my mother, Judi Warren, and my grandmother, Maria Tumilty. Their words of wisdom found their way into this book, as their influence has found its way into every breath I take. Here is a little bit about them. May you find inspiration in their lives.

Judi Warren lived an eclectic life. Working as a blues singer throughout her early 20s, she completed college and worked as a teacher, social worker, and eventually an ordained minister. A visionary in her own right, she started the School of Truth and formed an International Alliance of the Church of Truth. As she approached the middle of her life, her calling changed, and she sought to broaden her understanding of the world by studying Sufism and Zen Buddhism before training to become a Sensei. When she wasn't teaching or inspiring people with her worlds and heart, she was moving them with her art.

Maria Tumilty was an entrepreneur at a time when women did not assume that role. Helping to develop the field of corporate interior design, Maria worked for J.W. Robinson Co. for several decades, opening all of their Southern California stores. Prior to that, she developed and sold carved wooden shapes to be used as children's toys. She sold these during the Great Depression as a way to support her family. Eventually, a major toy manufacturer bought the idea and repackaged her wooden blocks. Maria was the epitome of a strong and inspirational woman throughout her life, influencing her daughter and granddaughter.

In addition to the advice from my mother and grandmother, many other women contributed to this book in some way through focus groups, questionnaires, and interviews. The following people went above and beyond to share a bit about themselves and their lives. I've included their bios in the hopes that they will inspire you as much as they have inspired me.

Rev. Mona Chicks is an ordained American Baptist pastor (retired), who supervises the home-based learning of her profoundly gifted and twice-exceptional son. She enjoys reading, writing, movies, and sports (playing and watching), and is a big fan of the Seattle Sounders FC (soccer) and Linfield College Wildcats (football). Mona writes about raising a profoundly gifted/twice-exceptional child on her blog, Life With Intensity. Mona and her family live in the state of Washington.

Paula Earl is the mother of two gifted sons who have stretched her intellect, challenged her creativity, and educated her more than any university ever did. Now that her sons are in college, she has turned her attention to working to positively impact our planet and its creatures with the Ian Somerhalder Foundation, focusing on one of the foundation's missions—engaging and supporting the world's youth. Paula has vowed to never stop learning and growing as a human being, to follow her passions, and to live life to the fullest.

Rebekah Graham lives in New Zealand with her husband, four children, and two cats. She is currently studying toward her master's degree in applied psychology and has a strong interest in social issues, in particular the way that culture influences the way in which social justice issues are perceived and resolved. Like many Kiwis, she enjoys spending time in the garden and growing fresh food for her family. She also volunteers with a local Community Fruit Organization that picks surplus fruit and redistributes it to families in need and local charities.

Erin Hastedt is a teacher and coordinator for the gifted program in Highlands Ranch, CO. Being labeled as a gifted student in her youth and raising two highly gifted children has fueled and driven her passion for advocacy and support of gifted programming. She feels that gifted students, like herself, are/were often misunderstood, underestimated, and/or labeled "weird" but works hard to help young minds think differently and have the confidence to be themselves, especially young girls. When she's not creating projects, testing students, or watching and marveling at her kids' many activities, she enjoys reading, running, and watching clever TV shows with her husband of 12 years.

Elle Horne has had a passion for great books since before she could walk. That passion developed into a deep-rooted desire to help bring amazing stories to the world. She is a talent scout for Compass Press and the publishing company's marketing director.

Stasia Ward Kehoe grew up dancing and acting on New England stages. She then moved to Washington, DC, and later New York, choreographing everything from theatrical productions to magic acts. She now lives with her husband and four sons in the Pacific Northwest. Her debut novel, *Audition*, was published with Viking/Penguin.

Jessi Kirby is the author of *Moonglass*, *In Honor*, and the forthcoming *Golden*. She is also a former English teacher and librarian, wife, mom, beach lover, runner, and lover of contemporary YA, strong coffee, and dark chocolate. In that order.

S. R. Johannes is the author of *Untraceable* (a teen wilderness thriller), its sequel, *Uncontrollable*, and the new tween romance, *On the Bright Side*. She has published short novelettes as well as a teen romance anthology with 16 other authors titled, *In His Eyes*. S. R. Johannes was recently nominated in the YA category as Georgia Author of the Year. She is also the 2012 winner of the IndieReader Discovery Awards for Young Adult.

Heather McCorkle is an author of fantasy, in all its many subgenres. Living green, saving endangered species, and helping other writers and supporting fabulous authors are a few of her passions. When she's not writing or surfing her social networking sites, she can be found on the slopes, on the hiking trails, or on horseback. As a native Oregonian, she enjoys the outdoors almost as much as the worlds she creates on the pages. Heather is also a volunteer for the Ian Somerhalder Foundation, which works to make the world a greener place.

Michelle McLean is the author of historical and paranormal romances and educational nonfiction, including *Homework Helpers: Essays and Term Papers* and *Treasured Lies*. She grew up in California and has lived everywhere from the deserts of Utah to the tropical beaches of Hawaii to the gorgeous forests of New England. She has a bachelor's degree in history, a master's degree in English, an insatiable love of books, and more weird quirks than you can shake a stick at. She currently resides in Pennsylvania with her husband and two young children, an insanely hyper dog, and two very spoiled cats.

Gretchen McNeil is an opera singer, writer, and clown. She's written two YA horror novels *Possess* and *Ten*. Her upcoming releases include *3:59* and the series *Don't Get Mad* (*Revenge* meets *The Breakfast Club*). Gretchen blogs with The Enchanted Inkpot and is a founding member of the vlog group the YARebels where she can be seen as "Monday."

Jen Merrill is a Chicago-based blogger and writer. After years of jamming her twice-exceptional son into various school settings that didn't quite fit, she's now a homeschooler and couldn't be happier. She loves saving documentaries into her Netflix queue, rolling her own sushi, and pretending she's still as good a flutist as she was back in the day (a.k.a. the advanced performance degree that was). When she has something to say, Jen says it at her blog, Laughing at Chaos. She's also the author of *If This Is a Gift, Can I Send It Back? Surviving in the Land of the Gifted and Twice-Exceptional*.

Abby Mohaupt is a pastoral intern at First Presbyterian Church in Palo Alto, CA, and the Faith Community Liaison at Puente de la Costa Sur in Pescadero, CA. She earned a bachelor's degree in religion and sociology from Illinois Wesleyan University in Bloomington, IL, and she did her seminary training at McCormick Theological Seminary, in Chicago, where she earned Master of Divinity and Master of Theology degrees. Her research and professional interests lie at the intersection of pastoral care with communities of people who have been marginalized and environmental theology. Abby and her partner, Nathan, live in Palo Alto, CA.

Lisa Rivero lives in Milwaukee, WI, where she is a writer and adjunct associate professor at Milwaukee School of Engineering. Some of her published books include *Creative Home Schooling*, *A Parent's Guide to Gifted Teens*, and *The Smart Teens' Guide to Living*

With Intensity: How to Get More Out of Life and Learning. She also writes the blog Creative Synthesis for *Psychology Today.*

B. E. Sanderson is a former single mom and past corporate "jack of all trades." She now lives the hermit's life in northeast Colorado, where she devotes her time to writing, reading, enjoying life with her husband, and helping her now-grown daughter survive early adulthood.

Melodye Shore vowed in third grade that she would grow up to be the kind of teacher she always wished she'd had—someone who took special notice of the kids who staked out positions along the beige back walls of an overcrowded classroom. Achieving that dream, Melodye taught disadvantaged and underprepared students in grades 7 through college. She now works as a freelance writer, editor, and speaker, with works appearing in publications such as *TIME* Magazine, the *Christian Science Monitor*, the *Los Angeles Times*, *Sports Illustrated*, and *USA Today*. In addition to writing, Melodye's interests include gardening, photography, and planning new adventures.